Snack Art

Written by Elizabeth Meahl
Illustrations by Barb Lorseydi
Cover Art by Sue Fullam

Teacher Created Materials

Teacher Created Materials, Inc.

6421 Industry Way

Westminster, CA 92683

© 1999 Teacher Created Materials, Inc.

Reprinted, 2000

Made in U.S.A.

www.teachercreated.com

ISBN #1-57690-318-4

Library of Congress Catalog Card Number: 99-070797

Editor:

Stephanie Buehler, M.P.W., M.A.

Table of Contents

Introduction 5

How to Use this Book 7

Safety in the Work Area 8

Food Restrictions 9

Foods to Use 10

Let's Go Shopping 12

Equivalent Ingredients 13

Weights and Measures 14

Comparing Labels 15

Help with Directions 16

After You Finish 18

Clean Up 19

Snack Art Faces 20

    Make a Face 22

    Creating the Snack Art 23

    Chef 25

    Clown 27

    Football Player 29

    Japanese Doll 31

    TV Character 33

Snack Art Animals 35

    Alligator 37

    Ant and Spider 39

Bat 41

Bear 43

Beaver 45

Bird 47

Buffalo 49

Butterfly 51

Cat 53

Caterpillar 55

Clam 57

Cow 59

Dog 61

Elephant 63

Fox 65

Frog 67

Giraffe 69

Goat 71

Hippopotamus 73

Horse 75

Koala Bear 77

Lamb 79

Leopard 81

Lion 83

Monkey 85

Table of Contents (cont.)

Mouse. 87

Opossum 89

Ostrich 91

Otter 93

Owl 95

Panda 97

Pig 99

Porcupine 101

Rabbit. 103

Raccoon 105

Rat 107

Rattlesnake 109

Seal 111

Turtle 113

Snack Art for All Seasons 115

Football 117

Halloween Alien 119

Thanksgiving Turkey. 121

Winter Reindeer 123

Snowman 125

Valentine's Day Muffin 127

Rainbow. 129

Flowers. 131

Baseball and Bat. 133

Bicycle. 135

Skateboard 137

Fish in Water 139

Snack Art Nutrition Activities 141

The Food Pyramid 143

Make Food Pyramid Placemats. 145

Go Eat: Food Pyramid Card Game 147

Celebrating Birthdays 151

Stick the Food on the Pyramid 152

Going on a Picnic 153

Peanut Butter and Ant Sandwich 153

Sandwich Tag 154

Stay Healthy with Sports 155

"Feed Me" Paper Bag Puppets. 156

Have Fun with Science Fiction 157

Moon Rock Cookies. 157

Mystery Label Game 158

Index of Recipes for Leftovers 159

Index for Snack Art 160

Introduction

Snack Art is both a recipe and a craft book. The central idea is to use food just as you would other craft material, then eat what you create.

The recipes in this book:

- Use familiar, healthy foods that are easily obtained.
- Provide a fun way to try new foods.
- Include suggestions for food substitutes.
- Have easy-to-follow directions.

There are a few things to keep in mind when using this book with children. For nearly all the recipes, you should allow children to assemble their own creations—their final product does not have to be an exact copy of the book illustration. In addition, you may find that some children will want to use the foods to make something completely different than what appears on the page. It's fine to encourage creative ideas. Substitutions for recipe ingredients are also acceptable (see page 10–11). The most important thing to remember is that these are fun activities that can help you create some warm family or group memories.

Introduction *(cont.)*

Art
colors

shapes

textures

creativity

Science
animals

body parts

food origins

senses

Nutrition
Food Pyramid

healthy eating habits

introducing new foods

Cooking
cutting

measuring

pouring

spreading

Math
counting

measurements

metric vs. U.S. measurements

portion sizes

money (shopping)

Language Arts
grocery lists

label reading

conversations about project

social skills

sharing

self-confidence

personal differences/
preferences

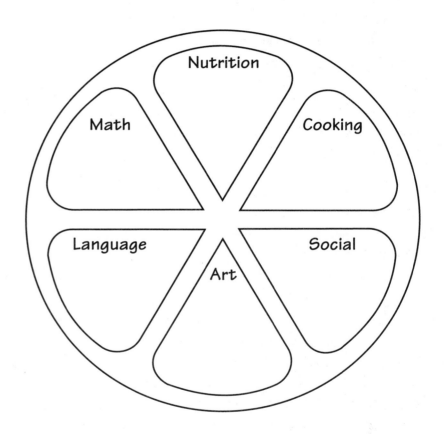

6

How To Use This Book

This book is very easy to use. Each snack is clearly illustrated with its parts labeled. The recipes on the "Creating the Snack Art" pages include an ingredient list and directions for assembly. Also included are ideas for substitutions and variations. Many recipes also include ideas for making use of leftover food.

Most recipes require only the use of a cutting board and a paring knife to prepare the foods for assembly. However, when softer foods such as bananas, bread, or strawberries are being prepared, feel free to make things easy by using heavy paper plates as individual cutting boards and plastic knives as cutting utensils.

Planning Ahead

If you are working with your own children at home in the kitchen, then you can just get the ingredients out and prepare everything together before you assemble the snack. Older children who are experienced in the kitchen may also be able to do their own preparation. Advance preparation is, however, a good idea when working with groups of very young children; older children with no cooking experience; groups with less than one adult per two to three children; working with very large groups; when time is limited; or when using recipes that require fine motor skills or experience with a knife

Tips for Working with Groups

Introduce cutting and other cooking skills gradually, after the children get used to working with the food. Recipes that require experience with a sharp knife are indicated, along with a note to refer back to this page.

Make it easy to follow directions by making copies of the illustration, then putting them in plastic sheet protectors and placing them on the table for each group.

Before you begin creating each snack, go over the following directions with the group:

- Read the recipe.
- Gather all the food items.
- Wash all fresh fruits and vegetables.
- Get out all the equipment.
- Wash your hands.
- Have a safe cooking experience!

Safety in the Work Area

Prevent Choking

Small pieces of food such as nuts, hot dogs, etc., may cause choking in small children. You can help prevent this danger by doing the following:

- provide adequate supervision

- enforce a strict no running, jumping, or rough playing rule around the work area

- continue activity only if children are seated and have adequate work space

- separate preparation time from eating time

Safety Checklist

☐ Have a clear, clean work area.

☐ Participants remain at their work spaces.

☐ Hands are washed with soap and warm water. Hands should be washed again after sneezing or coughing.

☐ Hair should be kept tied back.

☐ Adequate supervision must be provided.

☐ Knife use must be closely supervised by an adult.

☐ A cutting board must always be used to chop foods.

☐ Appliances are used by an adult or experienced older child.

☐ Appliances are unplugged when not in use.

☐ Use pot holders for hot foods.

☐ Clean up spills immediately.

Food Restrictions

Before starting a group cooking project, find out if anyone will be unable to eat the snacks because of food allergies or other dietary restrictions. You may want to send a letter, such as the one below, home with each child. If a child does have a food allergy or restriction, try to find a substitute food item either for the group or for that particular student.

- -

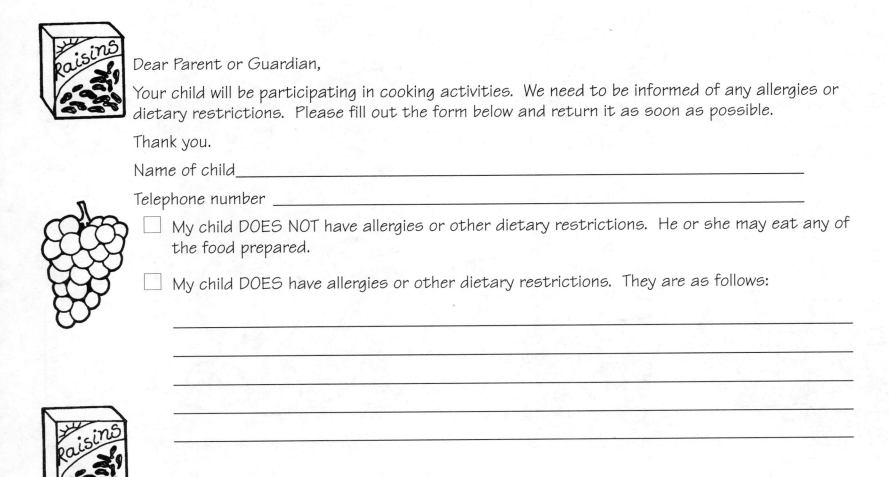

Dear Parent or Guardian,

Your child will be participating in cooking activities. We need to be informed of any allergies or dietary restrictions. Please fill out the form below and return it as soon as possible.

Thank you.

Name of child_____

Telephone number _____

☐ My child DOES NOT have allergies or other dietary restrictions. He or she may eat any of the food prepared.

☐ My child DOES have allergies or other dietary restrictions. They are as follows:

_____

_____

_____

_____

_____

Foods to Use

What if you want to make a snack but don't have all the foods listed in the recipe? Look for other foods that have similar sizes or shapes. See Help with Directions on page 16 for help with cutting directions.

Large Round Foods

bread   crackers   bagels   round fruit slices

Use for heads, faces, bodies, wheels, balls, etc. Cut to size and shape as needed.

Small Round or Oval Foods

raisins or
dried cranberries

dried apricots,
prunes, or bananas

grapes   blueberries   peas

cherry tomatoes,
tomatoes

black or stuffed
olive slices

Use for eyes, ears, mouth, nose, teeth, wheels, etc. Cut to size and shape as needed.

Foods to Use (cont.)

Be sure to use foods that taste good together. For example, blueberries and cream cheese are yummy together, but would you want to eat blueberries with liverwurst? Olives and liverwurst would be a better choice.

Long Thin Foods

cut carrots, cucumbers, green peppers, apples, or other vegetables and fruits

Short Thin Foods

grated carrots, cucumbers, apples, coconut, or other vegetables and fruits, grated cheese, shredded cereal

Use for hair, fur, manes, whiskers, eyebrows, quills, bicycle parts, etc. Cut to size and shape as needed.

Spreads

peanut butter

cream cheese

cheese spreads

meat spreads

Use for faces, bodies, or to add color or texture to art snacks.

Let's Go Shopping

Most of the recipes are for single servings. You will need to calculate the amount required for each ingredient.

1. From the recipe determine how much of a food is needed for one serving.

2. Multiply that amount by the number of servings you plan to make.

3. Compare the amount needed to how it is sold in the store (see page 13 for equivalents). For example, if you need 8 slices of bread, clearly you will have to get one loaf.

4. Make a grocery list. Include foods for the activity, possible substitutions, and other foods for recipes that use up the leftovers.

Grocery Worksheet				
Food Needed for 1 Serving X	Number of Servings =	Amount Needed	Compare to How It Is Sold in Stores (See page 13.)	Grocery List

Make copies of this worksheet to use for planning.

Equivalent Ingredients

Vegetables

carrots, 1 pound = 6.8 medium
1 medium = 20–30 round slices
cucumber, 1 pound = 3 medium
1 medium = 20–30 slices
mushrooms, 1 pound = approximately 30 medium
olives, 6 ounce can, large pitted = approx. 44 olives
tomatoes, 1 pound = 3 medium
1 medium = 6–8 slices

Fruits

apples, 1 pound = 3 medium
bananas, 1 pound = 2.3 medium
blueberries, 1 pound = 2 $\frac{1}{4}$ cup
grapes, seedless, 1 pound = 2 $\frac{3}{4}$ cup
lemons, 1 medium = 3 tablespoons juice
oranges, 1 medium = $\frac{1}{3}$ to $\frac{1}{2}$ cup juice
1 medium = 6–8 slices
pear halves, 16 oz. can = approx. 8 halves
prunes, 8 oz. pkg. = approx. 28 prunes
raisins, 1 pound = 3 cups loosely packed
strawberries, 1 pound = 3 cups

Nuts

almonds (shelled), 1 pound = 3 cups
peanut butter, 18 oz. jar = 30 tablespoons
pecans (shelled), 1 pound = 4 cups

Breads, Crackers, and Cereals

bread, 1 pound loaf = 14 to 20 slices
bread crumbs (fresh), 1 slice bread with crust = 1 $\frac{1}{2}$ cup crumbs
crackers, 14 oz. box = approx. 120 crackers
flour, 1 pound all-purpose = approx. 3 $\frac{1}{2}$ cups

Dairy Products

butter or margarine, $\frac{1}{4}$ pound = 1 stick = $\frac{1}{2}$ cup
cheese, $\frac{1}{4}$ pound = 1 cup shredded

Weights and Measures

Measurement Equivalents

1 tablespoon = 3 teaspoons

$\frac{1}{3}$ cup = 5 tablespoons + 1 teaspoon

1 cup = 16 tablespoons

1 quart = 4 cups

1 gallon = 4 quarts

1 pound = 16 ounces

Metric Conversions

United States customary measurement is used throughout this book. For metric conversions, use the following approximate amounts:

Weights

2.2 pounds = 1 kilogram (1,000 grams)

1 pound = 454 grams

1 ounce = 28.5 grams

Liquid measure

1 teaspoon = 5 milliliters

1 tablespoon = 15 milliliters

1 cup = $\frac{1}{4}$ liter

4 $\frac{1}{3}$ cup = 1 liter

Oven temperatures

Fahrenheit	Celsius
275°	135°
325°	163°
350°	177°
375°	190°
400°	204°
425°	218°
450°	232°

Linear measurements

1 inch = 2.54 cm

Comparing Labels

Read labels. Look for the list of ingredients, serving size, fat, sodium, fiber, vitamin, and mineral content.

Compare label of similar items. Look for higher %DVs for vitamins, minerals, and fiber. Look for lower %DVs for fat, sodium, and sugar.

(%DV = Percent Daily Value = the recommended amount for one person for one day, based on a 2,000 calorie-a-day diet.)

---

100 % Whole Wheat Bread   1 lb.

Nutrition Facts	Amount/serving	%DV	Amount/serving	%DV
Serving size: 1 slice (38g)	**Total Fat** 1g	2%	**Total Carbohydrate** 19g	6%
Serving per Container: 12	Saturated Fat 0g	0%	Dietary Fiber 3g	13%
Calories: 100	**Cholesterol** 0g	0%	Sugars 2g	
Calories from Fat: 10	**Sodium** 180mg	9%	**Protein** 3g	

Vitamin A 0% • Vitamin C 0% • Calcium 2% • Iron 6% • Thiamin 10% • Riboflavin 4% • Niacin 6% • Folic Acid 8%

INGREDIENTS: WHOLE WHEAT FLOUR, WATER, HIGH FRUCTOSE CORN SYRUP, WHEAT NUGGETS, YEAST, WHEAT GLUTEN, CONTAINS 2% OR LESS OF THE FOLLOWING: HONEY, SALT, MOLASSES, SOYBEAN OIL, RAISIN JUICE, YEAST NUTRIENTS, (AMMONIUM SULFATE), DOUGH CONDITIONERS (MONO & DIGLYCERIDES), VINEGAR.

White Enriched Bread   1 lb.

Nutrition Facts	Amount/serving	%DV	Amount/serving	%DV
Serving size: 1 slice (38g)	**Total Fat** 1.5g	2%	**Total Carbohydrate** 18g	6%
Serving per Container: 12	Saturated Fat 0g	0%	Dietary Fiber 1 g	3%
Calories: 101	**Cholesterol** 0g	0%	Sugars 2g	
Calories from Fat: 12	**Sodium** 220mg	9%	**Protein** 4g	

Vitamin A 0% • Vitamin C 0% • Calcium 6% • Iron 6% • Thiamin 10% • Riboflavin 6% • Niacin 6% • Folic Acid 10%

INGREDIENTS: ENRICHED FLOUR (FLOUR, BARLEY MALT, NIACIN, IRON, THIAMINE MONONITRATE, RIBOFLAVIN, FOLIC ACID), WATER, HIGH FRUCTOSE CORN SYRUP, YEAST, CONTAINS 2% OR LESS OF THE FOLLOWING: SALT, WHEAT GLUTEN, SOYBEAN OIL, DOUGH CONDITIONERS (MONO & DIGLYCERIDES), SUGAR, MILK, CORN FLOUR, VINEGAR, SOYA FLOUR, YEAST NUTRIENTS (AMMONIUM SULFATE).

These two labels are from bread.

- Which one has a higher DV for fiber? for vitamins and minerals?
- Which one has a lower DV for fat? for sodium?
- Which bread would you buy? Why?

For more fun with labels, see The Mystery Label Game on page 158

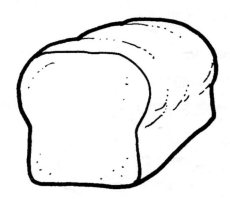

#2318 Snack Art

Help with Directions

Sometimes direction can be confusing because it is hard to visualize the process and result. Refer to these pictures when you are cutting foods to use for snack art.

Cut crosswise.

Cut lengthwise.

Help with Directions *(cont.)*

Cutting bread into rounds: Use a drinking glass or other round object that matches the size you want. Place rim side down on top of the bread. Cut around the rim with a knife.

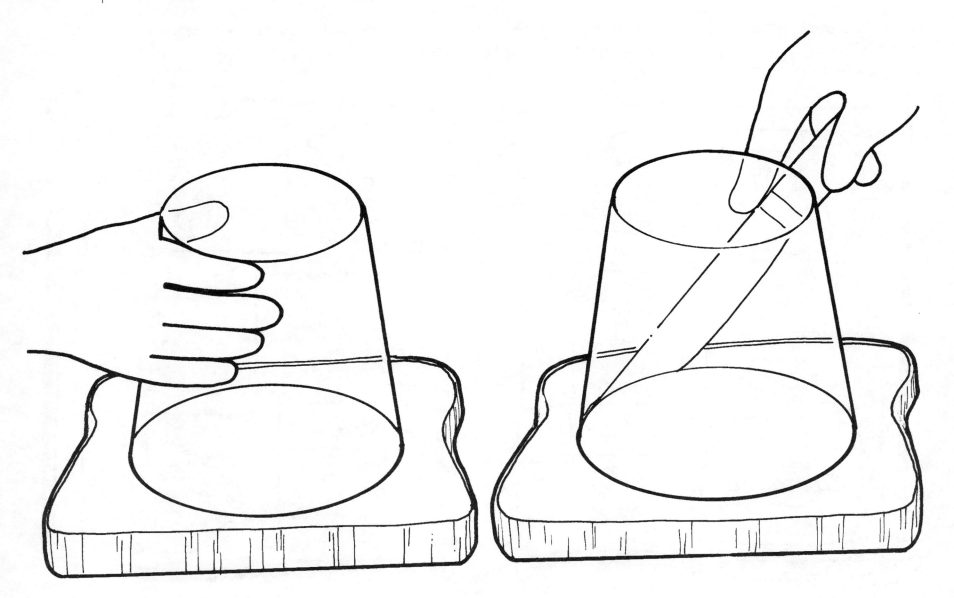

After You Finish

Take Pictures

You can't save your snack art, but you can save a picture. You might wish to buy or create a special small album to hold photos of snack art or of children making their creations. Label the photos and embellish the pages with comments about anything special that happened during the experience. Add appropriate stickers or make hand-drawn borders, if you wish.

Clean Up

1. Save scraps you can use later. (See Ideas for Leftovers on pages 158 and 159)			2. Throw away scraps you can't eat (peelings, pits, etc.).
3. Wipe the table with a clean cloth.			4. Set the table.
5. Wash your hands with soap and water after touching garbage and before eating.			6. Clear the table after eating.
7. Wipe the table with a clean cloth.			8. Throw away scraps you didn't eat and aren't going to save.
9. Throw away used paper goods.			10. Wash dishes.

Snack Art Faces

We all have hair, eyes, noses, ears, and mouths, yet everyone is unique.

Snack Art Faces (cont.)

Create an original face, copy one from here or on page 20, or try making "YOU."

Make a Face

Use these ingredients to create your snack art. Be sure to use foods that taste good together. For example: Cheddar cheese spread and olives go together while peanut butter and tomatoes don't go together.

Head: White, wheat, rye, or other bread or large round cracker

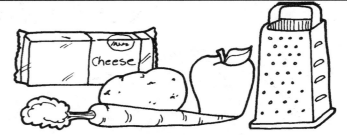

Straight hair: grated fruits, vegetables or cheese or cheese slice cut into hair shape

Skin: Peanut butter, cream cheese, cheese slice or spread, meat slice or spread

Eyes: blueberries, nuts, raisins, green peas, olives

Curly hair: toasted oat cereal, black olives cut crosswise, carrot curls, alfalfa sprouts

Mouth: red grape, cherry, dried cranberry, tomato edge slice, cherry tomato slice cut crosswise

Creating the Snack Art

Creating the Snack Art

INGREDIENTS

- white or dark bread or crackers
- peanut butter, cream cheese, cheese slice or spread, or meat slice or spread
- toasted oat cereal
- black olives
- grated cheese, fruit, and/or vegetables
- variety of fruit and vegetables chunks or pieces

UTENSILS

- cutting board
- round drinking glass, about 3" in diameter
- paring knife
- table knife
- grater

LET'S DO IT!

Note: The ingredients listed are possible suggestions. Pick and choose the ones that will help you create the face you wish to make. You may also be able to do this activity at home with ingredients you already have on hand.

1. Plan ahead. What type of face do you want to create?
2. Gather all the foods you will need.
3. If using bread, cut it into a circle using a glass as a guide; cover bread with your choice of spread, cheese or meat.
4. Assemble remaining ingredients according to your plan.

MORE IDEAS

<u>Braided hair:</u> arrange grated vegetables or cheese or slices olives to look like braids

<u>Eyebrows:</u> strips of carrot, olives pieces, or cereal

<u>Whites of eyes:</u> puffed rice cereal placed on either side of a blueberry, raisin, or green pea

<u>Sunglasses:</u> use two grapes or olives cut lengthwise for lenses and olive or grape pieces for remaining parts

<u>Mustaches:</u> arrange raisin, carrot, or olive slivers

<u>Nose:</u> cut a nose of cheese or meat, or use sunflower or other small seeds as nostrils

<u>Freckles:</u> wheat germ

<u>Collar:</u> arrange parts of pineapple ring slices or rows of berries, olives, nuts, seeds, etc.

See following pages for some special faces, or make up your own.

LEFTOVERS

<u>Animal companions:</u> Find an animal snack art recipe that uses the same ingredients. Also check the "Index of Recipes for Leftovers" on page 159.

Chef

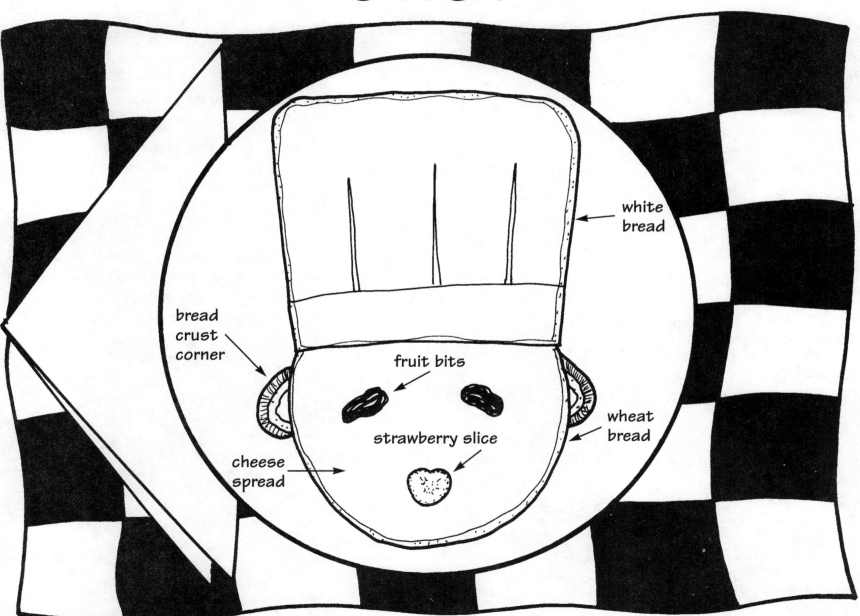

white bread

bread crust corner

fruit bits

strawberry slice

wheat bread

cheese spread

#2318 Snack Art

Creating the Snack Art

INGREDIENTS

- wheat bread
- slice of bread
- strawberry slice
- low-fat cream cheese spread
- fruit bits
- white bread

UTENSILS

- cutting board
- table knife
- paring knife

LET'S DO IT!

1. Cut head and hat shapes from bread as shown.

2. Spread top of bread slice with cream cheese.

3. Put "pleats" in hat, making 3 or 4 cuts in the bread as shown.

4. Use corners of leftover bread crust to make ears.

5. Add fruit bits for eyes and a strawberry slice for a mouth.

6. Assemble remaining ingredients as shown.

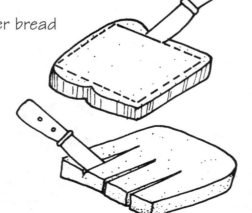

MORE IDEAS

- When you are ready to eat, fold the snack in half to make a sandwich.

- Make a "meaty" chef with white bread: Use a piece of luncheon meat cut to size for the face. Add olives for eyes and a small tomato slice for the mouth.

LEFTOVERS

Checkerboard sandwiches: Use one slice of white bread and one slice of whole grain bread. Add any desired filling. Cut sandwiches into quarters. Arrange quarters so that two are brown side up and two are white side up.

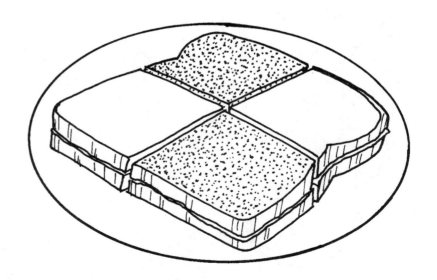

Clown

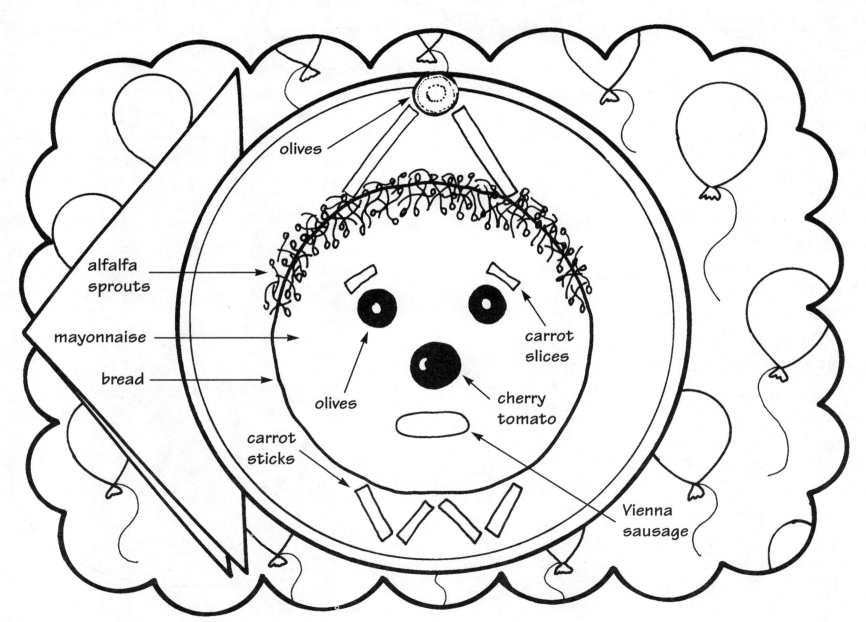

olives

alfalfa
sprouts

mayonnaise

bread

olives

carrot
sticks

carrot
slices

cherry
tomato

Vienna
sausage

27

Creating the Snack Art

INGREDIENTS

- bread slice
- mayonnaise
- handful of alfalfa sprouts
- several carrot slices
- olives bits
- one cherry tomato
- one Vienna sausage

UTENSILS

- cutting board
- round drinking glass, about 3" in diameter
- paring knife
- table knife

LET'S DO IT!

1. Cut bread into a circle, using glass as a guide.
2. Spread the bread with mayonnaise.
3. For nose, cut cherry tomato in half; place cut side down.
4. For mouth, cut sausage in two lengthwise. To create a smile, make tiny cuts along one side of sausage, and then bend sausage.
5. For collar, cut one edge off each carrot slice; place slices in a row under face. Place remaining ingredients.

MORE IDEAS

- Use grated carrots for orange hair.
- Make a fruit clown, using cream cheese as a spread. Look for colorful fruits to make eyes, nose, etc.

LEFTOVERS

Toothpick snacks: Cut Vienna sausages, olives and cherry tomatoes into bite-size pieces. Insert a toothpick in each and serve on a plate.

Football Player

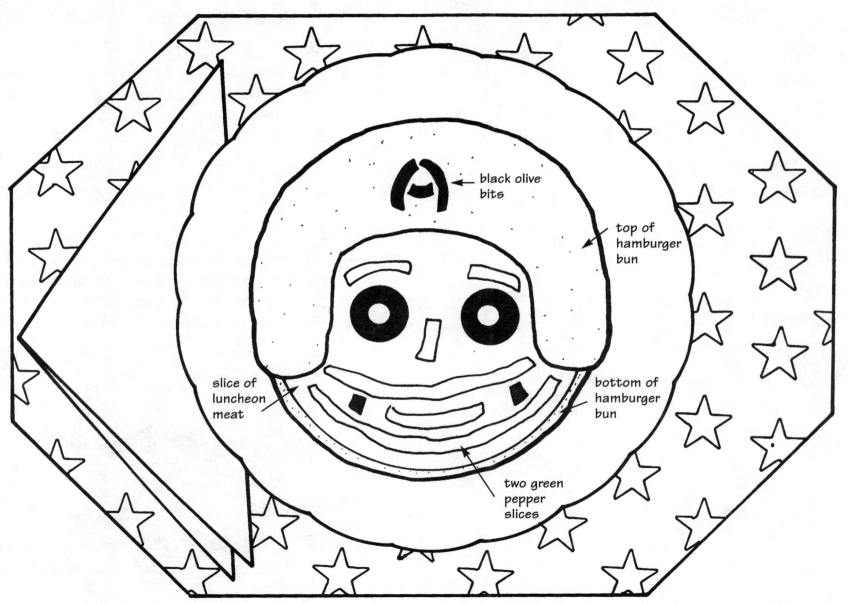

black olive bits

top of hamburger bun

slice of luncheon meat

bottom of hamburger bun

two green pepper slices

Creating the Snack Art

INGREDIENTS

- one hamburger bun
- one slice of luncheon meat
- mayonnaise or butter (optional)
- one or two black olives
- two slices of green pepper

UTENSILS

- cutting board
- paring knife
- table knife

LET'S DO IT!

1. Place bottom of hamburger bun on plate.

2. Spread bun with butter or mayonnaise if desired, then add luncheon meat.

3. Cut top of bun as shown, then place on top of player's head to make a helmet.

4. Add green pepper and olives to finish the snack.

MORE IDEAS

- Match the colors of favorite teams by using other cut vegetables instead of green pepper (e.g., red or yellow peppers, carrots, etc.).

- Use small strips of vegetables to draw an initial on the front of the helmet.

- See page 118 (Let's Do It!) to make a football.

LEFTOVERS

Jazzed-up hamburgers: Finely dice green pepper and make fine bread crumbs from unused buns. Mix with lean ground beef. Add salt, pepper, Italian seasoning, or other herbs and spices for more flavor. Grill or bake, then serve on buns.

Japanese Doll

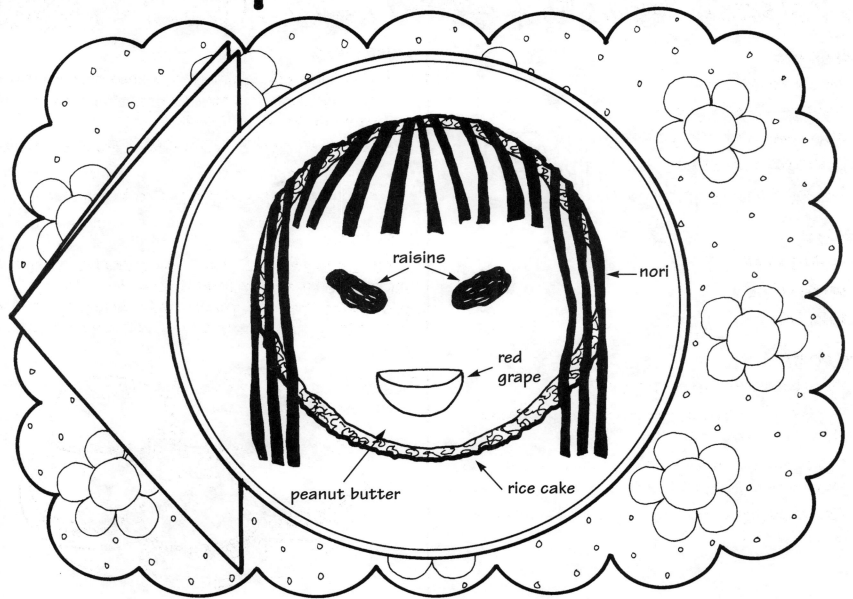

raisins

nori

red grape

peanut butter

rice cake

Creating the Snack Art

INGREDIENTS

- large rice cake
- peanut butter
- nori (see note)
- two raisins
- one red grape

UTENSILS

- cutting board
- kitchen shears
- paring knife
- table knife

LET'S DO IT!

1. Cut nori sheet into strands of hair with kitchen shears or paring knife.

2. To create a mouth, cut grape in half lengthwise, then cut one half into two pieces.

3. Spread rice cake with peanut butter and assemble snack as shown.

MORE IDEAS

Note: Nori is dried seaweed formed into thin sheets. It can be found in the Asian section of large supermarkets. If you can't find nori, you can make black hair using prunes. Cut prunes into long strips; arrange around face.

- You can also substitute other nut butters for peanut butter.
- Other appropriate fruits can stand in for eyes and mouth.

LEFTOVERS

<u>Rice cake snacks:</u> Serve rice cakes with a variety of toppings. Some suggestions are cream cheese, jam, and sliced fruit.

<u>Nori seasoning:</u> Crumble nori over steamed rice and vegetables in place of salt.

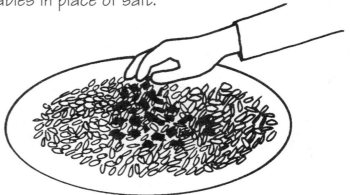

TV Character

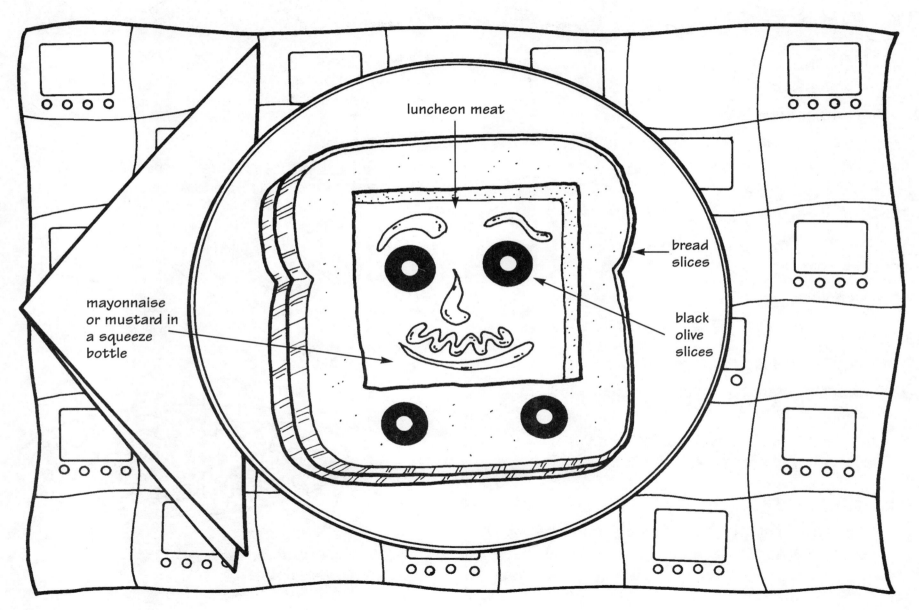

luncheon meat

bread slices

black olive slices

mayonnaise or mustard in a squeeze bottle

Creating the Snack Art

INGREDIENTS

- two bread slices
- several black olive slices
- mayonnaise or mustard in squeeze bottle
- luncheon meat

UTENSILS

- cutting board
- paring knife
- table knife

LET'S DO IT!

1. Place a slice of luncheon meat on bread.
2. Draw a small face on top of luncheon meat with mustard or mayonnaise.
3. Cut center out of second slice of bread as shown; place on top of first slice.

MORE IDEAS

- Make faces from other ingredients such as raisins, shredded carrots, etc.

- When you are ready to eat, "turn off" the TV by replacing the cut-out piece of bread; eat like a regular sandwich.

LEFTOVERS

<u>Luncheon meat flavor buds:</u> Chop luncheon meat into tiny pieces. Use for flavoring in salads or on cooked vegetables.

Snack Art Animals

Snack Art Animals

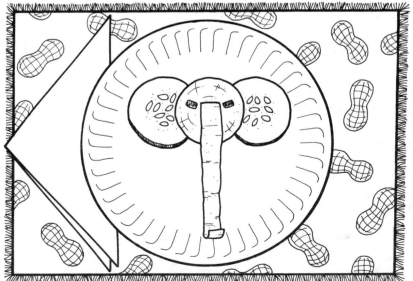

Alligator

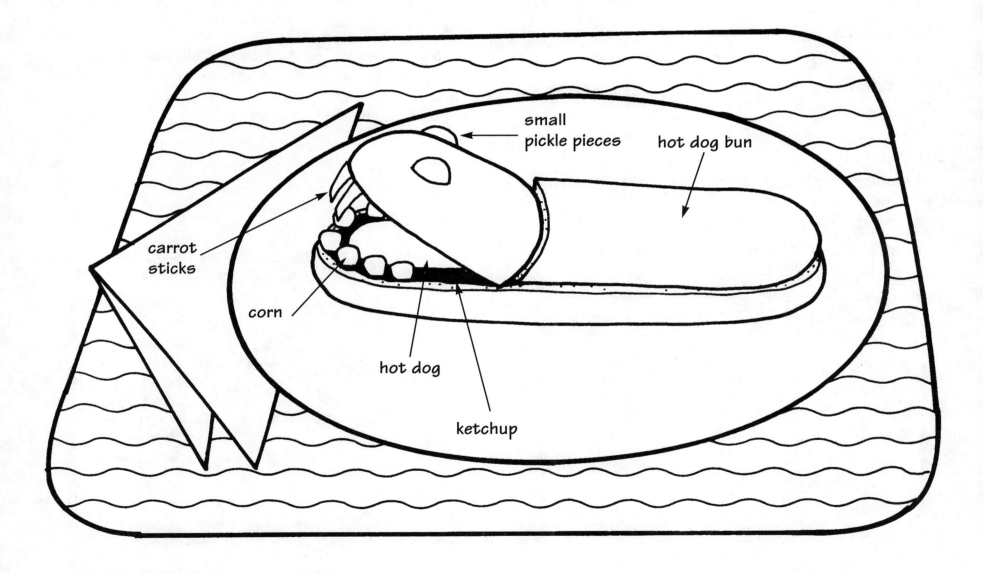

small pickle pieces

hot dog bun

carrot sticks

corn

hot dog

ketchup

Creating the Snack Art

INGREDIENTS

- hot dog bun
- ketchup
- several corn kernels
- hot dog
- two carrot sticks
- one pickle

UTENSILS

- cutting board
- paring knife
- table knife

LET'S DO IT!

1. Cut top half of bun in two crosswise. One piece will be the top of the head.

2. Spread a little ketchup on the bottom bun.

3. Cut hot dog in quarters as shown; place one quarter on bun.

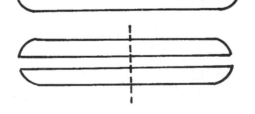

4. Add corn for teeth

5. Push two pointed carrot sticks into roof of mouth for fangs.

6. Cut ½" from the end of a small pickle. Cut this piece in two, place on top of bun for eyes.

MORE IDEAS

- Make a "sweet" alligator: Toast the hot dog bun. Spread the bottom half with red jam for the mouth. Use almonds for teeth, a bananas slice for the tongue, and green grapes for eyes.

- Find out the difference between alligators and crocodiles. Using a world map, point out where each lives.

LEFTOVER

<u>Beans with corn and hot dogs:</u> Mix a can of baked beans with leftover corn and sliced hot dogs. Heat and serve.

Ant and Spider

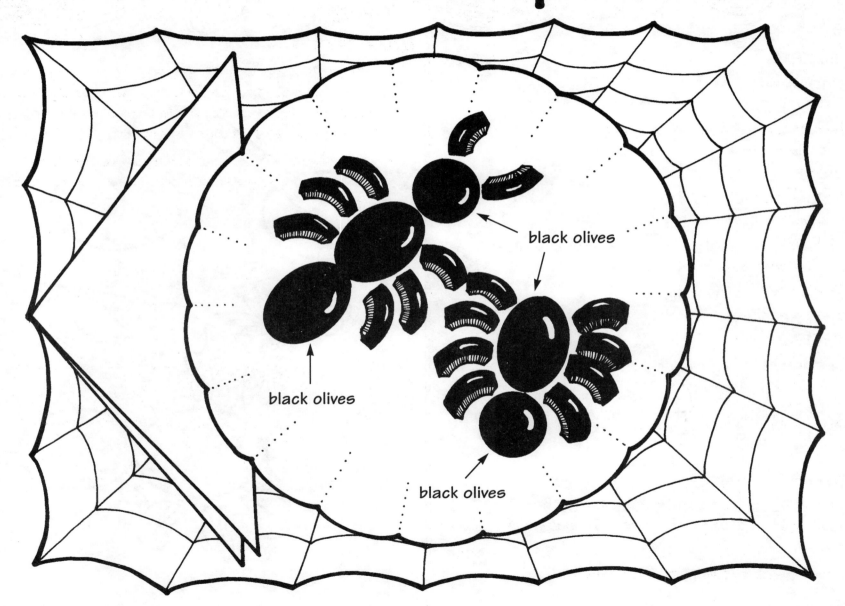

black olives

black olives

black olives

Creating the Snack Art

INGREDIENTS

- black olives

UTENSILS

- cutting board
- paring knife

LET'S DO IT!

1. Cut olives crosswise for head, lengthwise for body.

2. Cut olives crosswise into slices, then cut slices in half for legs.

3. Assemble pieces as shown.

MORE IDEAS

- Use grapes instead of olives to make the insects.

- Go outside or visit a park and look for different kinds of ants. Notice how they are alike and how they differ.

LEFTOVERS

Cheese and sliced olive sandwiches: Make cheese sandwiches. Add sliced black olives. These sandwiches taste good grilled.

Bat

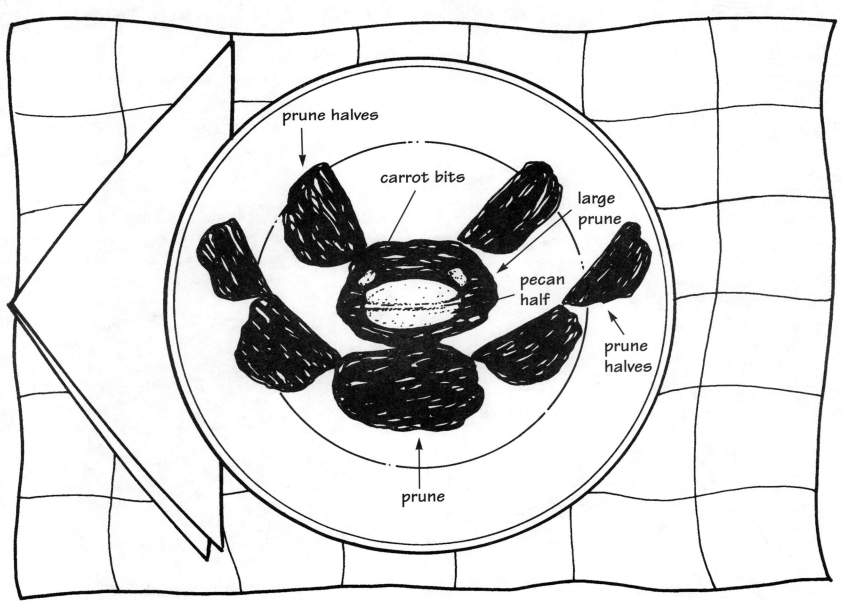

prune halves

carrot bits

large prune

pecan half

prune halves

prune

Creating the Snack Art

INGREDIENTS

- four prunes
- one carrot cut into bits
- pecan half

UTENSILS

- cutting board
- paring knife

LET'S DO IT!

1. Use one prune for body of bat.
2. Cut another prune in half crosswise for ears.
3. Cut two more prunes in half crosswise for wings.
2. Add remaining ingredients as shown.

MORE IDEAS

- To use fewer prunes, slice each prune thinly through the center to make two flat, round pieces.
- Find out about bats. Are bats really blind? How do they find their way around?

LEFTOVERS

<u>Oatmeal cookies with prunes and carrots:</u> Add ¼ to ½ cup chopped prunes and one small grated carrot to your favorite oatmeal cookie recipe. (See "Moon Rock Cookies" on page 157 for an oatmeal cookie recipe if you don't have one.)

Bear

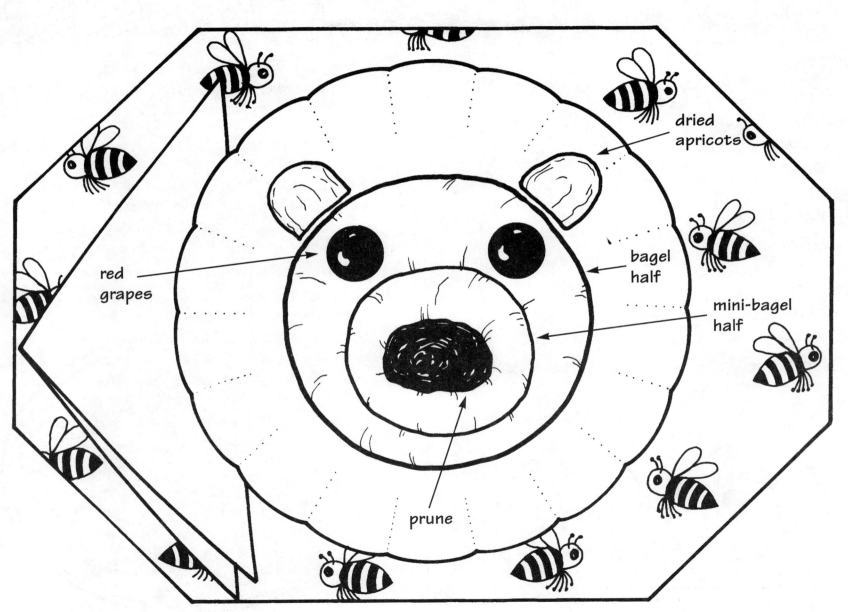

dried
apricots

bagel
half

red
grapes

mini-bagel
half

prune

#2318 Snack Art

Creating the Snack Art

INGREDIENTS

- one half regular bagel
- one half mini-bagel
- one red grape
- one prune

UTENSILS

- cutting board
- paring knife

LET'S DO IT!

1. Place the large bagel half flat side down on plate.

2. Place the mini-bagel half on top of large bagel, also flat side down, to create a snout.

3. Add remaining ingredients as shown.

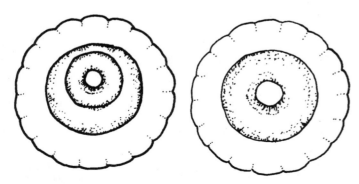

MORE IDEAS

- Use a strawberry half instead of a prune for the nose. Use cream cheese as "glue".

- If you can't find mini-bagels, cut a regular bagel smaller or use a small roll.

- Make your own "bear" dough. Follow a recipe for yeast rolls, then use one round piece for the face and a smaller for the nose. Flatten slightly before putting in the oven. Add the eyes, nose, etc. after baking.

- Make Goldilocks and the Three Bears: The bear as created in the recipe can be Papa Bear. For Mama Bear, put a flower on her ear, using grape pieces. For Baby Bear, make a head with mini-bagel or small round piece of bread, grape halves for ears, raisins for eyes and a small prune or prune piece for the snout. Act out the story when you have finished making the snack art.

LEFTOVERS

<u>Bagel snack:</u> Top bagels with cream cheese and chopped fruit.

Beaver

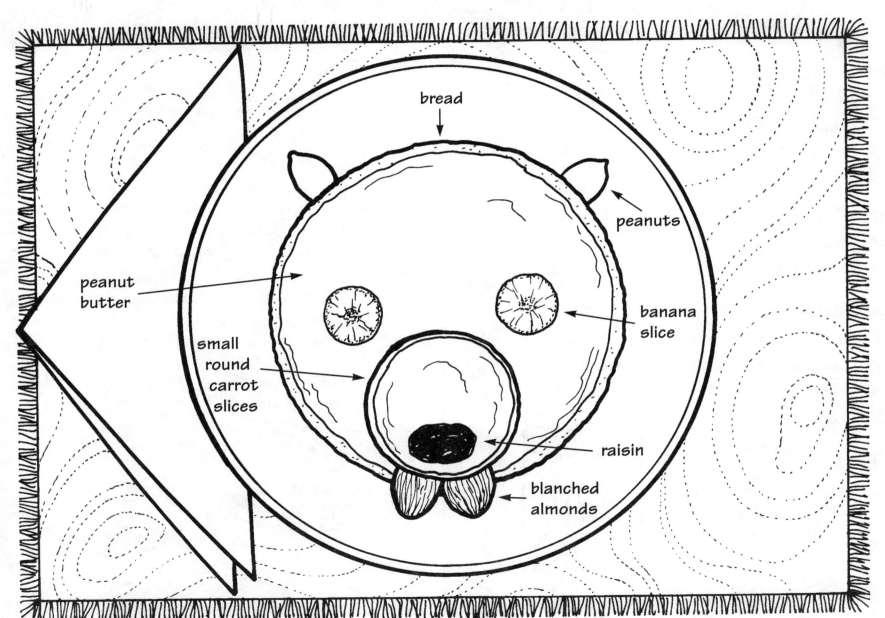

bread

peanuts

peanut butter

banana slice

small round carrot slices

raisin

blanched almonds

45

#2318 Snack Art

Creating the Snack Art

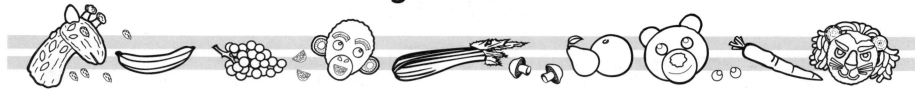

INGREDIENTS

- one slice bread
- peanut butter
- two peanuts
- carrot slices
- banana slice, 1/4" thick
- raisin
- two blanched almonds

UTENSILS

- cutting board
- round drinking glass, about 3" in diameter
- paring knife
- table knife

LET'S DO IT!

1. Cut bread into a round shape, using the glass as a guide.
2. Spread bread with peanut butter
3. Assemble as shown.

MORE IDEAS

- Make a beaver dam, using carrots cut into small sticks.

- Have a nut-tasting class. Learn about nuts. Look up nut recipes.

LEFTOVERS

Tuna patties: Mix one 6-oz. can drained tuna, 2 tablespoons bread crumbs, 2 tablespoons grated carrot, 1 tablespoon finely chopped almonds, and 1 beaten egg. Form into 4 patties and fry in small amount of oil.

Bird

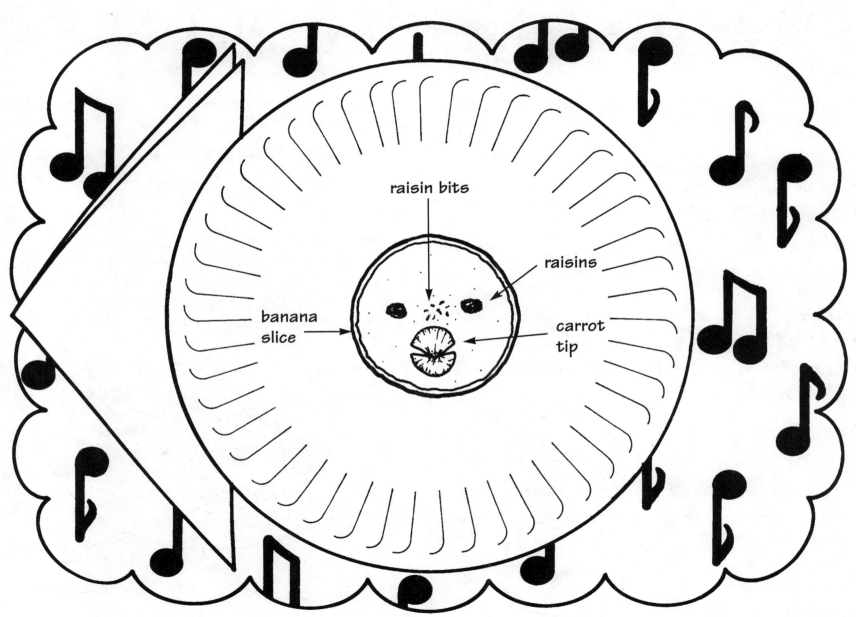

raisin bits

raisins

banana slice

carrot tip

#2318 Snack Art

Creating the Snack Art

INGREDIENTS

- one banana slice, 1/4" thick
- one raisin, quartered
- one carrot

UTENSILS

- cutting board
- paring knife

LET'S DO IT!

1. Cut 1/2" from pointed end of carrot; slice through the point lengthwise.
2. Place carrot pieces on the banana as illustrated.
3. Add raisin eyes.

MORE IDEAS

- Sprinkle lemon juice on banana to prevent browning.
- Use a round carrot slice instead of banana.
- Make a side-view bird; cut carrot beak into a pointed shape.

- Go on a walk. Look for birds. Draw pictures of the birds you see.

LEFTOVERS

<u>Banana pudding:</u> Make pudding as directed on box or recipe. Stir in sliced bananas. Add raisins and serve with whipped topping, if desired.

Buffalo

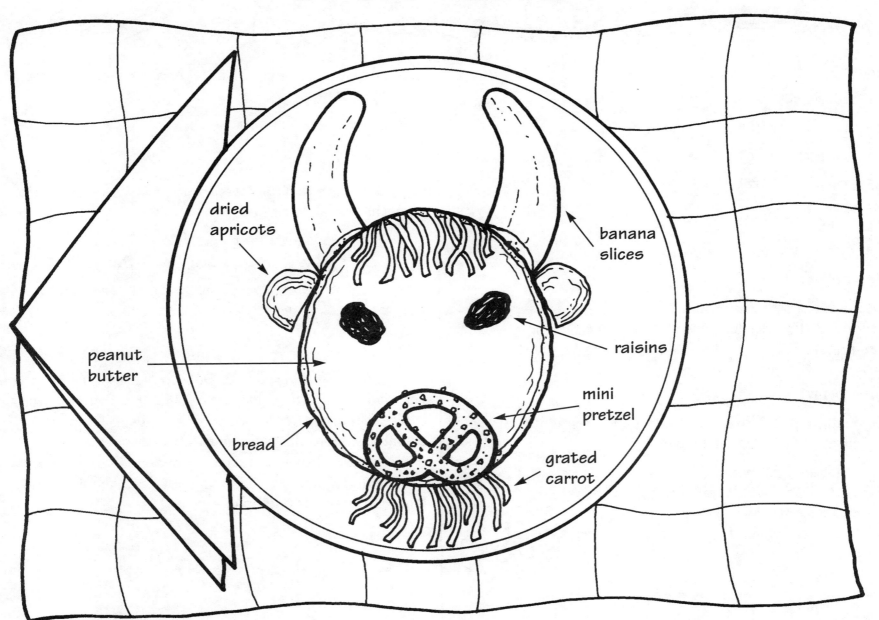

dried
apricots

banana
slices

peanut
butter

raisins

mini
pretzel

bread

grated
carrot

#2318 Snack Art

Creating the Snack Art

INGREDIENTS

- bread slice
- grated carrot
- one dried apricot
- one mini pretzel
- peanut butter
- one banana
- two raisins

UTENSILS

- cutting board
- table knife
- paring knife

Note: This recipe requires fine motor skills and experience. Prepare ingredients ahead of time, if needed. (See page 7.)

LET'S DO IT!

1. Remove crust from bread and cut bread into an oval. Spread with peanut butter.

2. Cut bananas in half crosswise, then in half again lengthwise. Use two of the curved lengthwise pieces for horns.

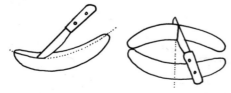

3. For ears, cut apricot in two crosswise; use ½ of an apricot for each ear.

4. Assemble as shown.

MORE IDEAS

- Use shredded carrots or shredded fresh apple for the buffalo's beard.

- Use carrot slices for ears.

- Look for books about buffalos in the library. Find out why there aren't as many buffalo in the United States as there were 200 years ago.

LEFTOVERS

<u>Meat Loaf:</u> Add bread crumbs and grated carrot to your favorite meat loaf recipe or try this one: Preheat oven to 350°. Mix together ½ pound ground beef; 1 cup bread crumbs; 2 beaten eggs; one 8 oz. can tomato sauce; ½ cup shredded raw vegetables; ½ teaspoon salt; and black pepper and/or other spices to taste. Bake mixture in large loaf pan for one hour.

Butterfly

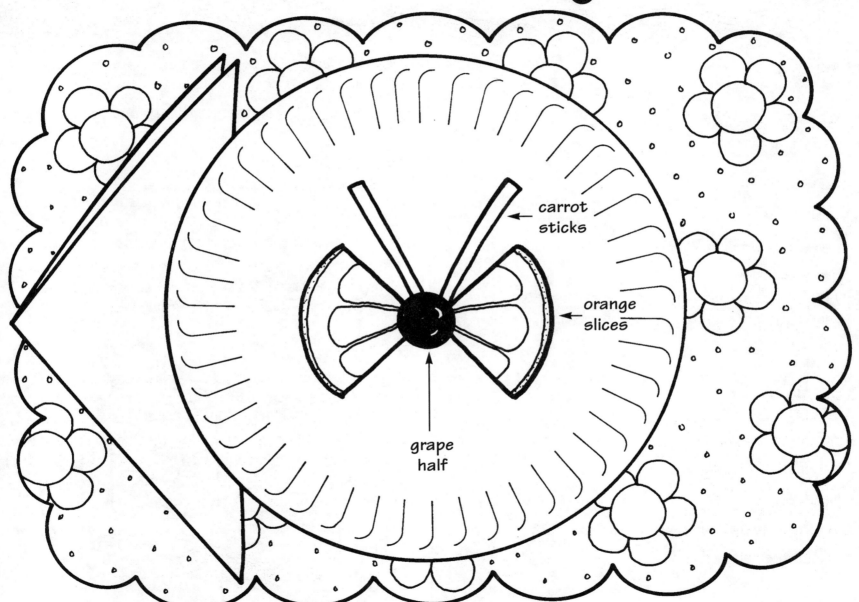

carrot
sticks

orange
slices

grape
half

#2318 Snack Art

Creating the Snack Art

INGREDIENTS

- one grape
- two carrot match sticks
- one orange slice

UTENSILS

- cutting board
- large knife to cut orange
- paring knife

Note: This recipe requires fine motor skills and experience. Prepare ingredients ahead of time, if needed. (See page 7.)

LET'S DO IT!

1. Cut orange crosswise; use 2 quarter slices per butterfly.
2. Assemble as shown.

MORE IDEAS

- Use any vegetable sticks for antennae.
- Make grapefruit butterflies.

- Make lemon butterflies to use as a garnish for fish, salad, or ice tea.
- Add a design to the wings with cut-up fruit pieces.

LEFTOVERS

<u>Fresh-squeezed orange juice:</u> Cut orange in half. Push into citrus juicer, or peel orange and put fruit into an electric juicer. Use the fresh juice in a smoothie with other fruits and some vanilla frozen yogurt or low-fat ice cream.

Cat

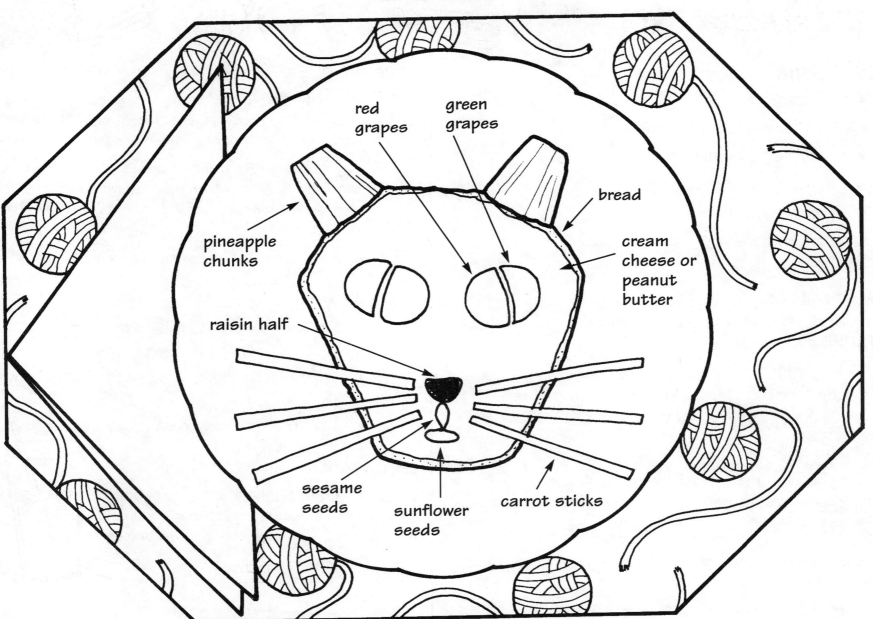

red grapes

green grapes

bread

pineapple chunks

cream cheese or peanut butter

raisin half

sesame seeds

sunflower seeds

carrot sticks

#2318 Snack Art

Creating the Snack Art

INGREDIENTS

- bread slice
- cream cheese or peanut butter
- two pineapple chunks
- one green and one red grape
- one raisin
- carrot match sticks
- sunflower seeds
- sesame seeds

UTENSILS

- cutting board
- round drinking glass, about 3½" in diameter
- paring knife
- table knife

Note: This recipe requires fine motor skills and experience. Prepare ingredients ahead of time, if needed. (See page 7.)

LET'S DO IT!

1. Cut bread into a circle, using the glass as a guide. Cut strips from both sides to make a cat-shaped face. Spread with cream cheese or peanut butter.

2. For eyes, cut green grape in two lengthwise; cut red grapes into slivers. Make a slit down the center of each green grape half and insert red grape slivers into slits.

3. Assemble remaining ingredients as shown.

MORE IDEAS

- For an easier version, use raisins or plain grape slices for eyes.
- Make a strawberry mouse (see page 87) to eat with the cat.
- Have a contest to see who can make the best meow.

LEFTOVERS

Carrot and raisin salad: Combine two grated carrots (about 1 cup), ⅓ cup raisins and ⅓ cup pineapple. Stir in 1–2 tablespoons mayonnaise. Chill before serving.

Caterpillar

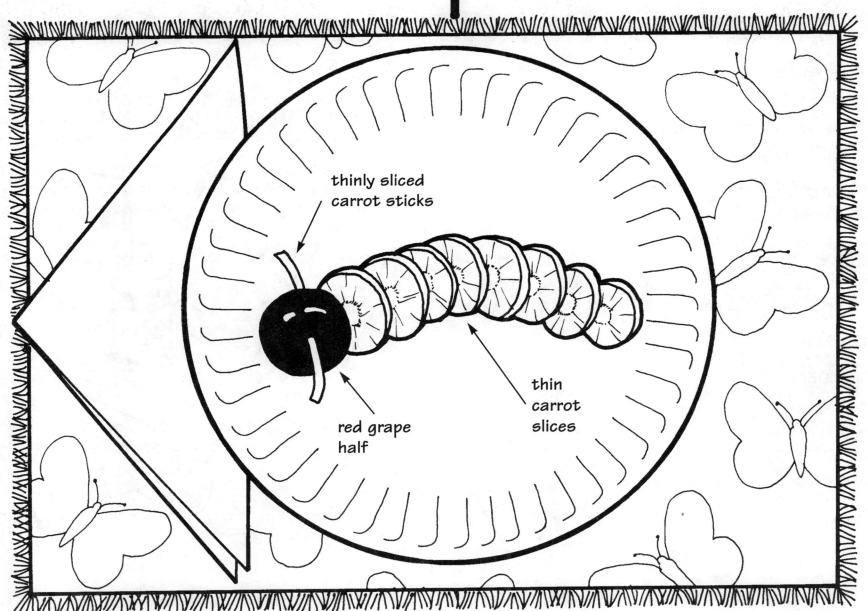

thinly sliced
carrot sticks

red grape
half

thin
carrot
slices

#2318 Snack Art

Creating the Snack Art

INGREDIENTS

- one red grape
- two carrot matchsticks
- carrot slices

UTENSILS

- cutting board
- paring knife

LET'S DO IT!

1. Poke carrot sticks into grape; you may need to pierce the grape with a sharp toothpick first.

2. Assemble as shown.

MORE IDEAS

- Use other veggie rounds instead of carrots.
- Make caterpillars (see page 52) and butterflies.
- Go to the library and look for a video that shows the transformation of a caterpillar to a butterfly.

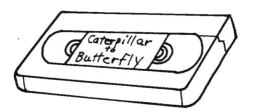

LEFTOVERS

<u>Carrot chips and pink dip:</u> Mix portions of low-fat mayonnaise, chili sauce, and relish to taste. Cut the whole carrot into round chips to dip.

Clam

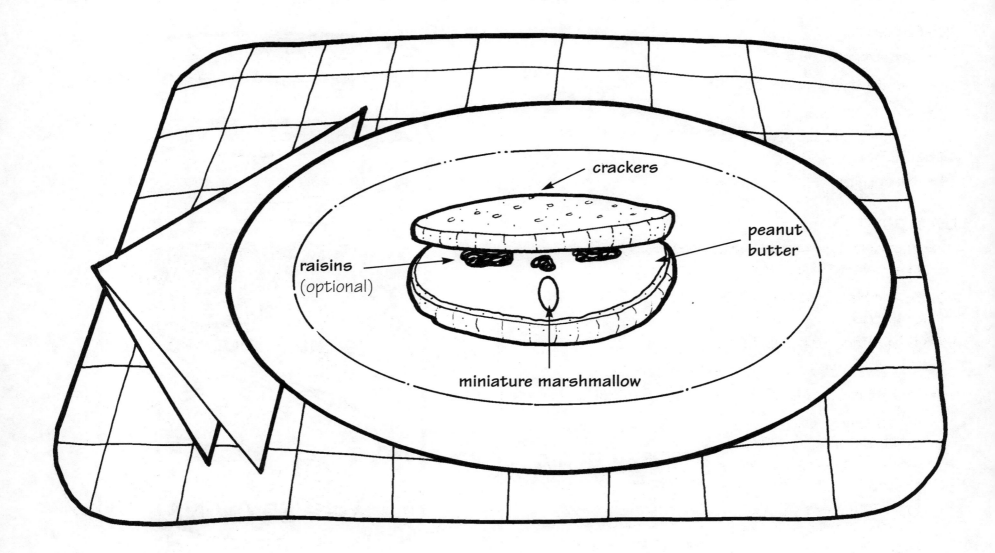

crackers

peanut butter

raisins (optional)

miniature marshmallow

#2318 Snack Art

Creating the Snack Art

INGREDIENTS

- two oval crackers
- peanut butter
- miniature marshmallow (optional)

UTENSILS

- table knife

LET'S DO IT!

Assemble as shown. Add a miniature-marshmallow pearl, if desired.

MORE IDEAS

- Add a face with raisin bits and sunflower seeds.
- Taste real clams, perhaps from a can.

LEFTOVERS

Supremely chunky peanut butter: Chop up seeds, raisins, and nuts. Stir into peanut butter to make your own unique spread.

Cow

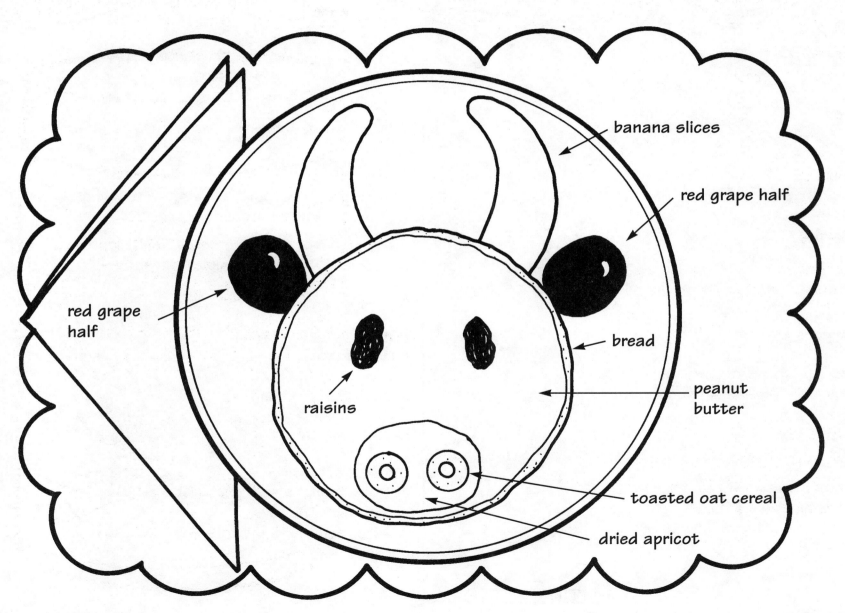

banana slices

red grape half

red grape half

bread

raisins

peanut butter

toasted oat cereal

dried apricot

Creating the Snack Art

INGREDIENTS

- bread slice
- one red grape
- one dried apricot
- two pieces toasted oat cereal
- peanut butter
- two raisins
- banana slices

UTENSILS

- cutting board
- round drinking glasses, about 3" in diameter
- paring knife
- table knife

Note: This recipe requires fine motor skills and experience. Prepare ingredients ahead of time, if needed. (See page 7.)

LET'S DO IT!

1. Cut bread into a circle, using the glass as a guide. Spread with peanut butter.

2. Cut bananas in half crosswise, then in half again lengthwise. Use two of the curved lengthwise pieces for horns.

3. Assemble remaining ingredients as shown.

MORE IDEAS

- Put some sprouts around the cow's head to symbolize the grass it eats.
- Serve milk with your cows. Talk about where milk comes from. If possible visit a dairy farm or a dairy.

LEFTOVERS

<u>Frozen bananas:</u> Freeze bananas rolled in a little sugar (1 teaspoon per banana). Use in recipes calling for bananas.

<u>Banana milk:</u> Blend $\frac{1}{2}$ frozen banana with one cup of milk. Pour over toasted oat cereal as a summer time breakfast.

Dog

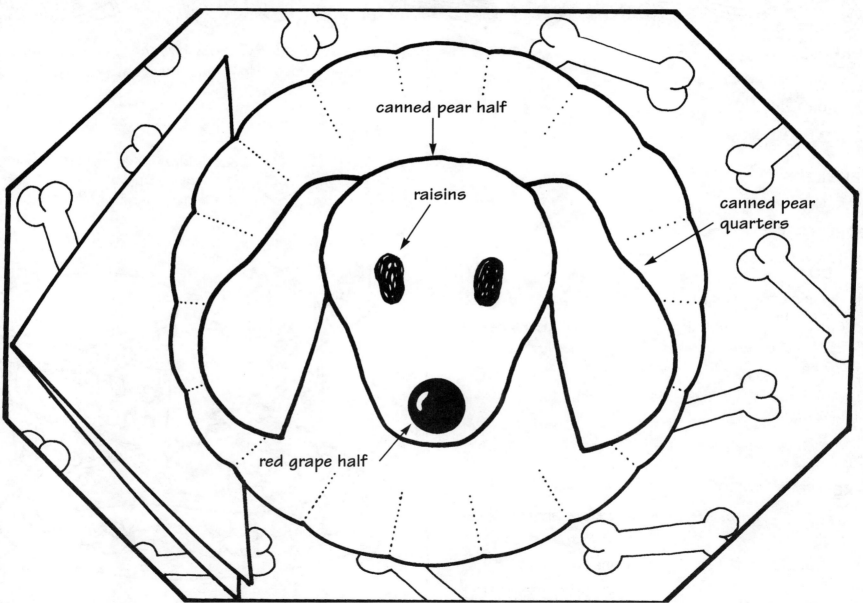

canned pear half

raisins

canned pear quarters

red grape half

Creating the Snack Art

INGREDIENTS

- two canned pear halves
- two raisins
- one red grape

UTENSILS

- cutting board
- paring knife

LET'S DO IT!

1. Place one pear half hollow-side down for face.

2. Cut other pear half in two lengthwise and place hollow-side down on either side of the dog's face for its ears.

3. Cut grape in two crosswise for a round nose, lengthwise for an oval nose.

5. Assemble as shown.

MORE IDEAS

- Use fresh pears; peel and core before arranging as described.
- Put spots on the dog with raisins.

- Conduct a survey to see how many children have dogs for pets. How many have cats or other animals?

LEFTOVERS

<u>Pear and cottage cheese salad</u>: Make a salad by filling pear halves with cottage cheese. Sprinkle with raisins and/or grapes. Serve on a lettuce leaf.

Elephant

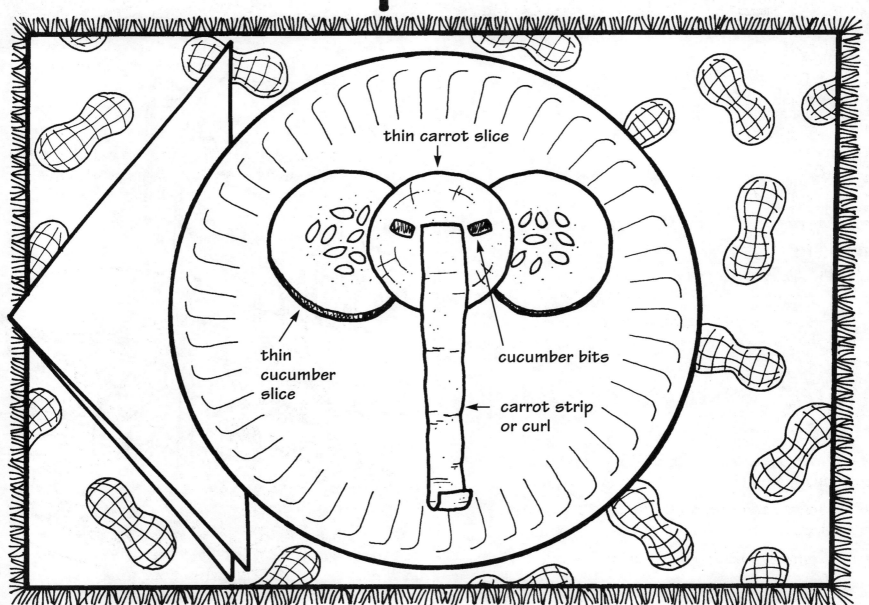

thin carrot slice

thin cucumber slice

cucumber bits

carrot strip or curl

Creating the Snack Art

INGREDIENTS

- one carrot
- one cucumber

UTENSILS

- cutting board
- paring knife

LET'S DO IT!

1. Thinly slice carrot and cucumber.
2. Create a carrot curl, using a thin strip.
3. Assemble as shown.

MORE IDEAS

- Use small cucumber slices for head.
- Use long carrot slice, with peel left on, for trunk.
- Talk about size. This elephant is very small; real ones are very large.
- Visit a zoo to see real elephants.

LEFTOVERS

Tuna dip: Mix together one 6 ½ oz. can tuna; ½ cup cottage cheese; and ¼ cup shredded carrots, cucumbers or other vegetables. For a smoother dip, mix in blender or food processor. Eat dip with cut vegetables or spread it on crackers or bread.

Fox

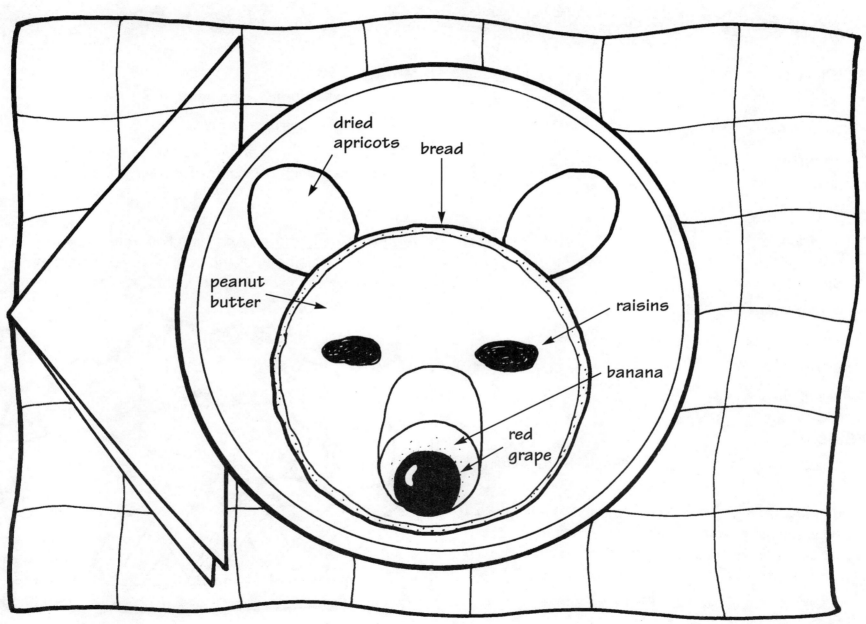

dried
apricots

bread

peanut
butter

raisins

banana

red
grape

#2318 Snack Art

Creating the Snack Art

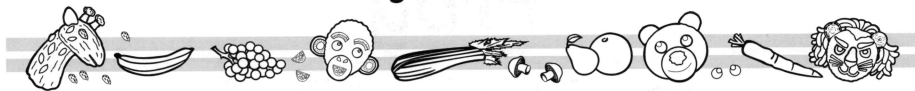

INGREDIENTS

- bread slice
- peanut butter
- two raisins
- one banana
- one red grape
- two dried apricots

UTENSILS

- cutting board
- round drinking glass, about 3" in diameter
- paring knife
- table knife

LET'S DO IT!

1. Cut bread into a circle, using the glass as a guide. Spread bread with peanut butter.

2. Cut banana in half crosswise, then in half lengthwise. Use one of the quarters as a nose, placing it cut-side down on the peanut butter so that it appears to jut from the face.

3. Assemble remaining ingredients as shown.

MORE IDEAS

- Use extra large grape halves for ears.

- Add thin carrot stick whiskers.

- Make other forest animals like bears, beavers, owls and raccoons (see index for page numbers).

LEFTOVERS

Additions to muffins: Add 1 medium mashed banana and ¼ cup each raisins and dried apricots to a plain muffin recipe. Decrease liquid in recipe by 2 tablespoons.

Frog

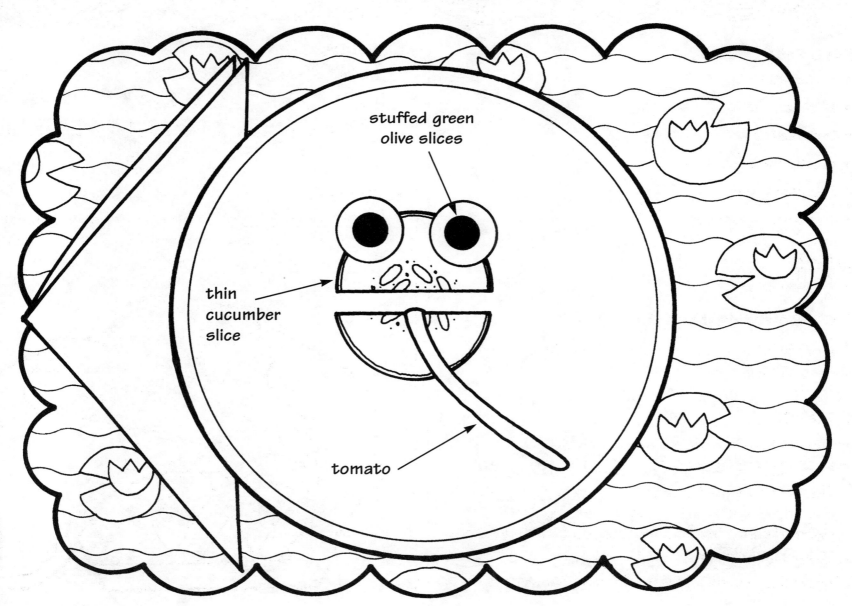

stuffed green
olive slices

thin
cucumber
slice

tomato

#2318 Snack Art

Creating the Snack Art

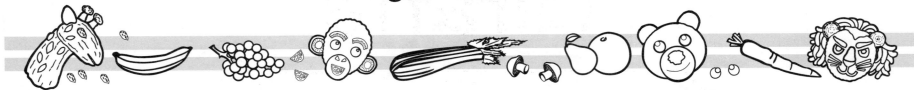

INGREDIENTS

- one cucumber
- one or two stuffed green olives
- one tomato

UTENSILS

- cutting board
- paring knife

LET'S DO IT!

1. Thinly cut a slice of cucumber. Cut slice nearly in half and separate slightly to create mouth.

2. Thinly cut a slice of tomato. Cut the edge of the slice. Use this edge as a tongue.

2. Slice olives and place them as eyes.

MORE IDEAS

- Make tadpoles: Cut a black olive in half lengthwise, then cut little pieces off each side to form the tail.

- Look up frogs in the encyclopedia or other resource book. Learn how tadpoles turn into frogs.

- Make a "sweet frog," using a kiwi slice for the head, an apple peel or red fruit strip for the tongue, and seeded grape slices for eyes.

LEFTOVERS

Cucumbers and dip: Cut cucumbers and tomatoes into slices. Eat with dip. (See page 56 for one idea.)

Giraffe

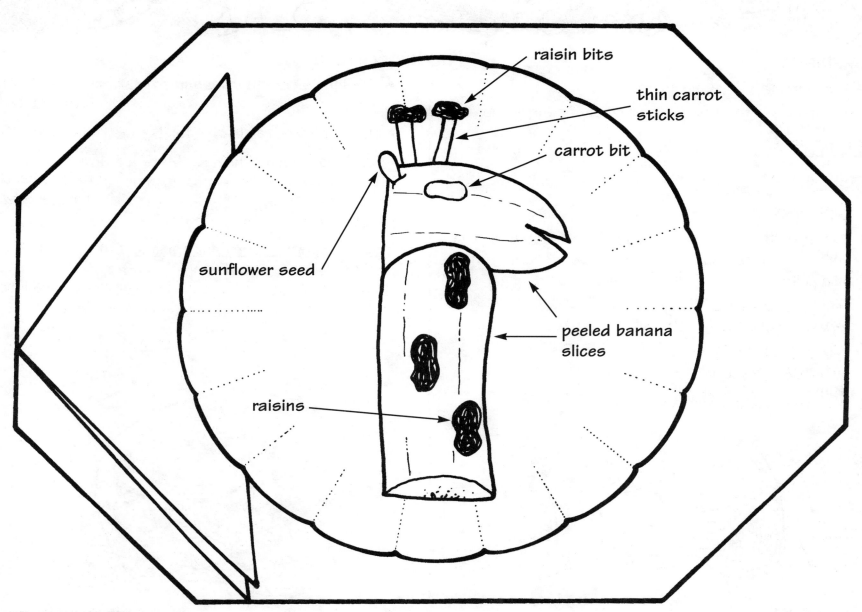

raisin bits

thin carrot sticks

carrot bit

sunflower seed

peeled banana slices

raisins

#2318 Snack Art

Creating the Snack Art

INGREDIENTS

- one banana
- raisins
- one carrot
- two unshelled sunflower seeds

UTENSILS

- cutting board
- paring knife

LET'S DO IT!

1. To make the head and neck: Peel banana and slice in half lengthwise. Cut one of the halves 1" inch from the pointed end to make the head. Cut a longer piece for the neck and place it flat side down on the plate.
2. Cut a small slit in the head for a mouth.
3. Assemble remaining ingredients as shown, using sunflower seeds for ears and raisins as spots.

MORE IDEAS

- Use long, straight bananas to make the neck really long.
- Use carrot or raisin bits for ears.
- Talk about animal height. Make a mural or draw pictures of tall and short animals.

LEFTOVERS

Banana slices with honey and raisins: Cut banana in slices; add raisins. Drizzle honey over all. Add nuts if desired.

Goat

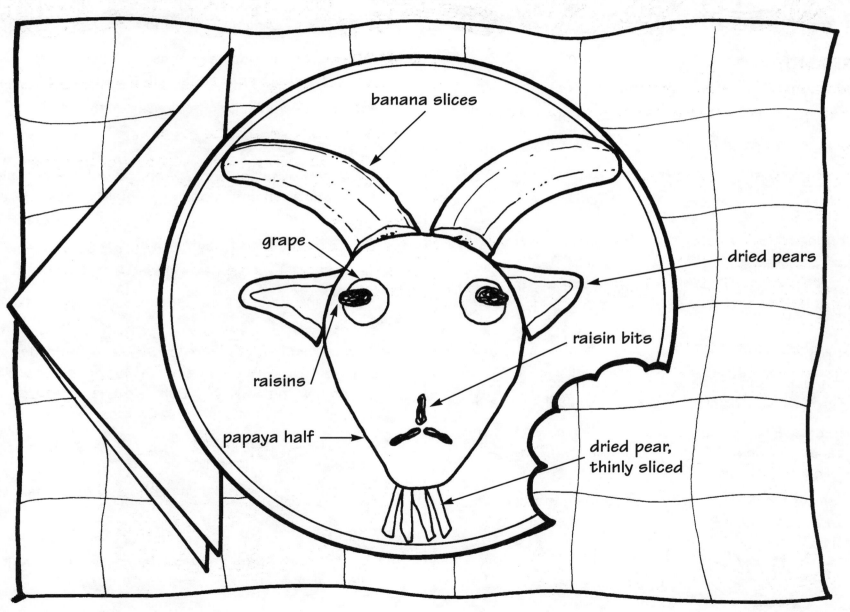

banana slices

grape

dried pears

raisins

raisin bits

papaya half

dried pear,
thinly sliced

#2318 Snack Art

Creating the Snack Art

INGREDIENTS

- one papaya
- banana
- one or two dried pears
- one grape
- two raisins

UTENSILS

- cutting board
- paring knife

Note: This recipe requires fine motor skills and experience. Prepare ingredients ahead of time, if needed. (See page 7.)

LET'S DO IT!

1. Cut papaya in half lengthwise and remove seeds. Pare away outer skin. Place papaya hollow side down.

2. To create horns, cut 3" from the curved end of the banana, then cut this piece in half lengthwise, following the curve.

3. For eyes, cut grape in two lengthwise; make a slit down the center of each half. Insert raisins into slits.

4. Cut dried pears into ear shapes. Thinly slice remaining dried pear to use as the goatee.

5. Assemble remaining ingredients as shown.

MORE IDEAS

- For a somewhat easier version, cut a large oval piece of bread for the head and use smaller banana slices for the horns.

- Use any shredded fruit for the goatee.

- To easily make eyes, use raisins.

- Use peanut butter or cream cheese as "glue" to attach ears, eyes, etc.

- To eat: remove eyes, ears, etc. To eat the other papaya half, turn papaya over, remove seeds, and scoop fruit out with a spoon. Or pare off the skin and cut papaya into bite-size pieces.

- Make a goat from bread, using the Let's Do It! directions for making the buffalo on page 50.

- Find out if goats really eat cans and other garbage.

LEFTOVERS

<u>Fruit shake:</u> Blend banana, papaya, frozen vanilla yogurt, and milk together in a blender or food processor.

Hippopotamus

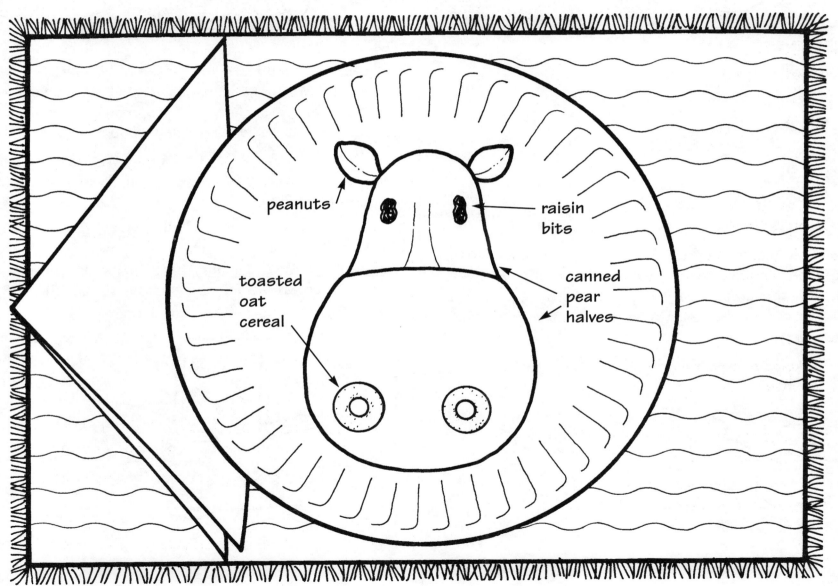

peanuts

raisin bits

toasted oat cereal

canned pear halves

73

#2318 Snack Art

Creating the Snack Art

INGREDIENTS

- one canned pear half
- two shelled peanuts
- two raisins
- two pieces toasted oat cereal

UTENSILS

- cutting board
- paring knife

LET'S DO IT!

1. Cut pear half in two crosswise. Place small end hollow side up to form the top of the face; place larger piece hollow side down to form the bottom of the face.

2. Assemble remaining ingredients as shown.

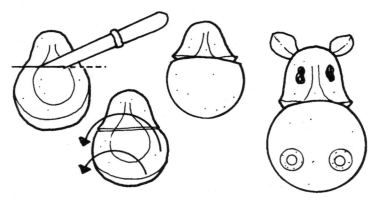

MORE IDEAS

- One day ahead, prepare plates of blue gelatin. Make gelatin according to package and pour into plates that have a lip. Assemble hippo on gelatin after it has set. It will look like the hippopotamus is looking at you from the water.

- Find out where the hippopotamus lives. Find these areas on a map.

LEFTOVERS

Pears with brown sugar and raisins: Sprinkle canned pears with brown sugar and cinnamon. Add raisins if desired.

Horse

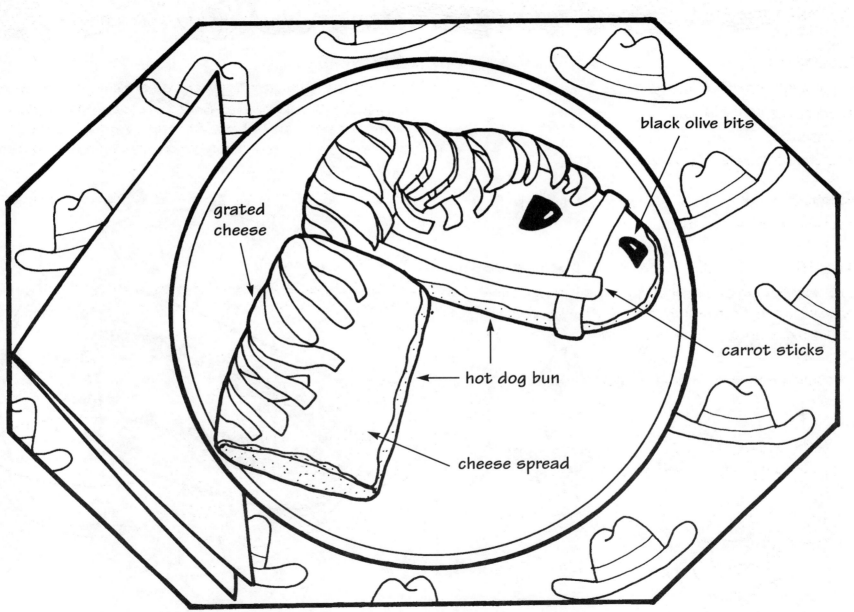

black olive bits

grated cheese

carrot sticks

hot dog bun

cheese spread

#2318 Snack Art

Creating the Snack Art

INGREDIENTS

- hot dog bun
- cheese spread
- black olives
- carrot sticks
- grated white or yellow cheese

UTENSILS

- cutting board
- paring knife
- table knife

LET'S DO IT!

1. Cut bun into two pieces as shown; place flat side up.

2. Cover with cheese spread and other ingredients.

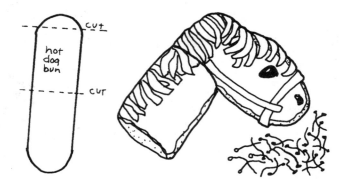

MORE IDEAS

- Put some sprouts by the horse's mouth to represent hay or grass.

- Have galloping races outside.

LEFTOVERS

Chili dogs with grated cheese: Heat canned or homemade chili in pan or microwave. Cook hot dogs in boiling water or microwave. Put hot dogs in buns. Top with 1 to 2 tablespoons hot chili. Sprinkle grated cheese and sliced olives on top.

Koala Bear

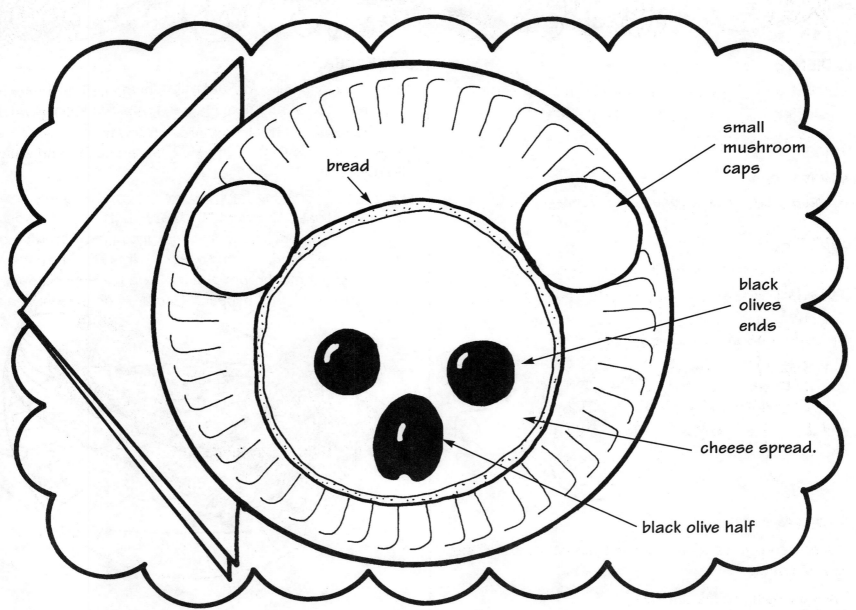

bread

small mushroom caps

black olives ends

cheese spread.

black olive half

#2318 Snack Art

Creating the Snack Art

INGREDIENTS

- bread slice
- cheese spread
- two mushroom caps
- three black olives

UTENSILS

- cutting board
- round drinking glass, about 3" in diameter
- paring knife
- table knife

LET'S DO IT!

1. Cut bread into a circle, using glass as a guide. Spread bread with cheese spread.
2. Cut ends off two black olives; use as eyes.
3. Cut one black olive in half lengthwise; use as nose.
4. Wash mushrooms and cut off stem.
5. Assemble as shown.

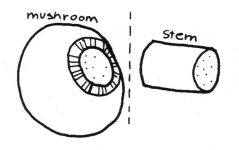

MORE IDEAS

- Koala bears live in Australia. Find Australia on a map. Learn about other Australian animals.
- Try some Australian foods like kiwi fruit.

LEFTOVERS

<u>Bread crumb coating for fish or chicken:</u> Make dry bread crumbs by toasting bread in toaster until it just starts to turn brown. Let cool, then tear into bread crumbs or whirl bread in blender. Mix together dry bread crumbs, finely chopped mushroom and olives, a little Parmesan cheese, and salt and pepper. Use as a coating for baked fish or chicken.

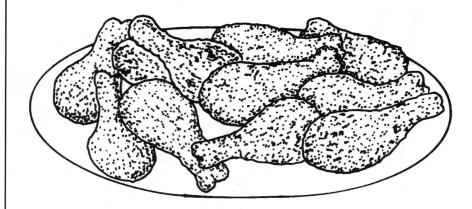

Lamb

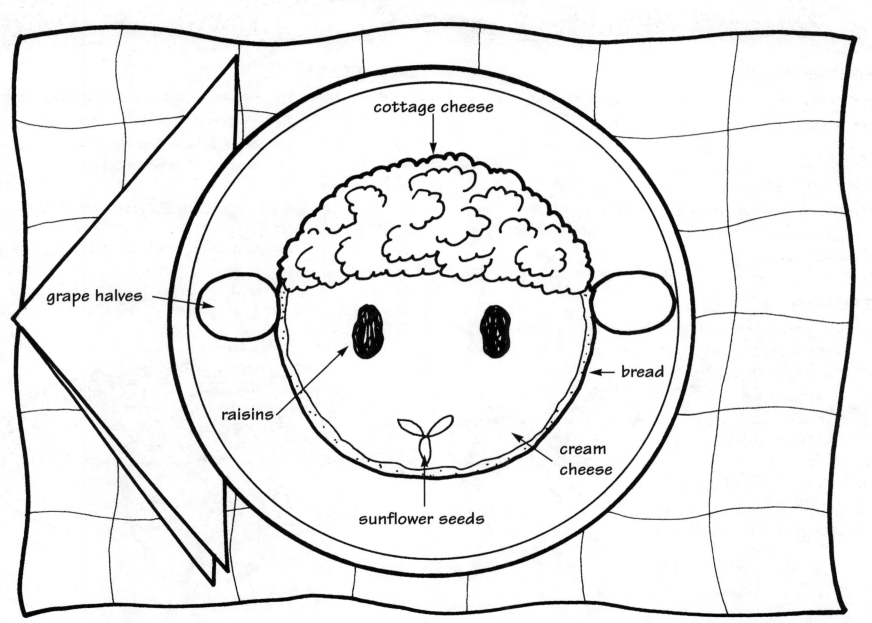

cottage cheese

grape halves

raisins

bread

cream cheese

sunflower seeds

#2318 Snack Art

Creating the Snack Art

INGREDIENTS

- bread slice
- cream cheese
- one grape
- two raisins
- shelled sunflower seeds

UTENSILS

- cutting board
- round drinking glass, about 3" in diameter
- paring knife
- table knife

LET'S DO IT!

1. Cut bread into a circle, using the glass as a guide. Spread bread with cream cheese.

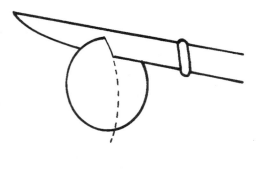

2. Cut grape in half lengthwise to use as ears.

3. Assemble ingredients as shown.

MORE IDEAS

- Make other farm animals, like cows (page 59) and horses (page 75).

- Recite "Mary Had a Little Lamb." Talk about fleece. Find out if anyone is wearing something made from wool.

LEFTOVERS

Cottage cheese and fruit parfait: Mix cottage cheese with a little cream cheese. Layer in cottage cheese mixture and grapes in clear glass. Sprinkle top with sunflower seeds, if desired.

Leopard

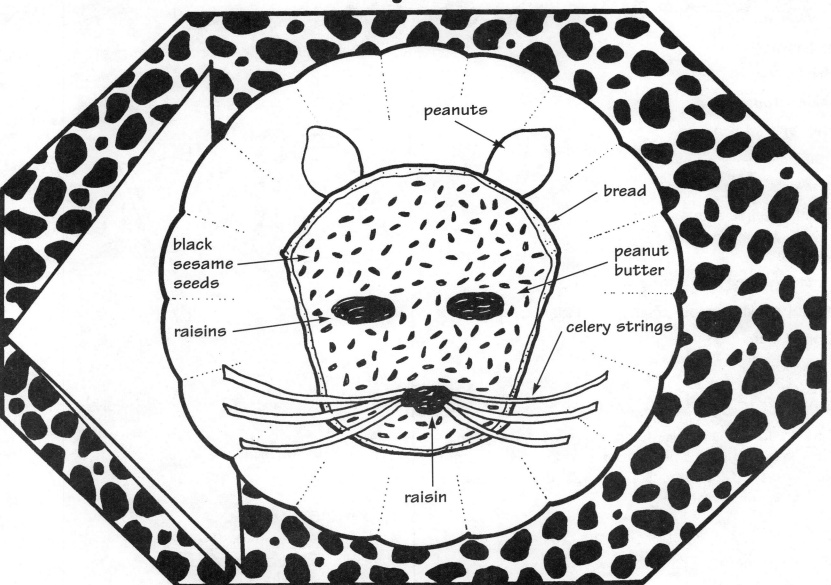

peanuts

bread

black
sesame
seeds

peanut
butter

raisins

celery strings

raisin

#2318 Snack Art

Creating the Snack Art

INGREDIENTS

- bread slice
- peanut butter
- two shelled peanuts
- raisins
- one celery stalk
- black sesame seeds

UTENSILS

- cutting board
- round drinking glass, about 1³/₄" in diameter
- paring knife
- table knife

LET'S DO IT!

1. Cut bread into a circle, using the glass as a guide. Cut small strips from both sides of the bread round to make the face more leopard-like. Spread bread with peanut butter.

2. For whiskers, peel strings from a stalk of celery; cut to desired size.

3. Add remaining ingredients as shown.

MORE IDEAS

- Make a big leopard using a large piece of bread and raisins as spots.
- Make a list of all the different kinds of cats, large and small.

LEFTOVERS

Addition to homemade bread: Find a recipe for homemade raisin bread or use a recipe for plain bread and add raisins to the dough.

Lion

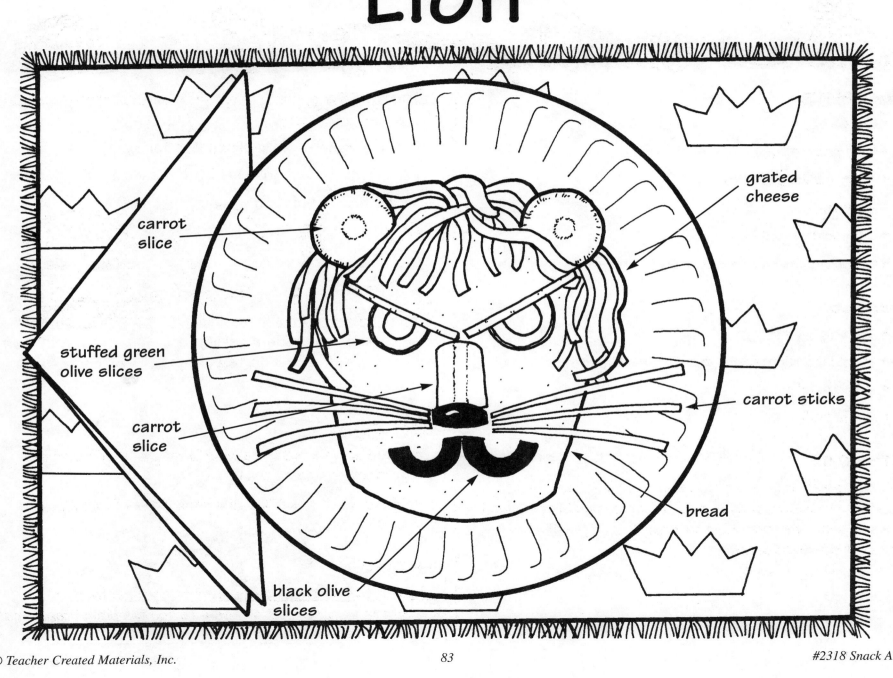

carrot slice

grated cheese

stuffed green olive slices

carrot slice

carrot sticks

bread

black olive slices

#2318 Snack Art

Creating the Snack Art

INGREDIENTS

- bread slice
- one carrot
- black olive slices
- grated white or yellow cheese
- one stuffed green olive

UTENSILS

- cutting board
- round drinking glass, about 3" inches in diameter
- paring knife
- table knife

Note: This recipe requires fine motor skills and experience. Prepare ingredients ahead of time, if needed. (See page 7.)

LET'S DO IT!

1. Cut bread into a circle, using the glass as a guide; cut small strips from both sides of the bread round to make the face more lion-like.

2. For eyes, cut stuffed olive slice in half; use 2 $\frac{1}{2}$ for each eye.

3. For mouth, cut olive crosswise into slices, then cut slices in half.

4. Add remaining ingredients as shown.

MORE IDEAS

- For an easier version, skip the eyebrows and nose; use round stuffed olive slices for eyes.

- Use grated carrots instead of cheese for the mane.

- Make a female lion without the mane.

- Find out why the lion is called the "King of the Jungle".

LEFTOVERS

Broccoli topped with bread crumbs and grated cheese: Put cooked broccoli in a baking pan. Top with a thin layer of bread crumbs and grated cheese. Place under broiler just until cheese melts.

Monkey

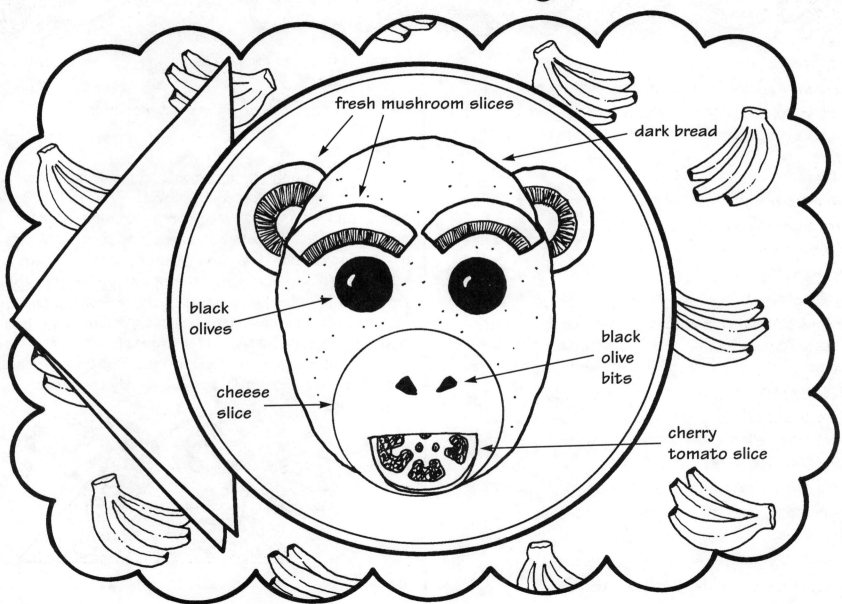

fresh mushroom slices

dark bread

black olives

black olive bits

cheese slice

cherry tomato slice

#2318 Snack Art

Creating the Snack Art

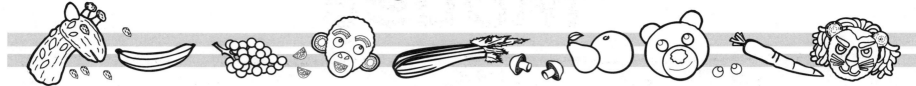

INGREDIENTS

- one slice dark bread
- one cherry tomato
- black olive bits
- one mushroom
- two black olives
- one cheese slice

UTENSILS

- cutting board
- paring knife

LET'S DO IT!

1. Remove bread crust and cut bread into oval shape.

2. Cut cheese slice to fit bread and place on top.

3. Remove stem from mushroom and discard. Slice mushroom crosswise; use two slices for the ears. Cut another mushroom slice in two for the eyebrows.

4. For mouth, cut cherry tomato crosswise.

5. Assemble ingredients as shown.

MORE IDEAS

- If you can't find cherry tomatoes, cut a piece of tomato to size. Use mayonnaise to "glue" cheese to face.

- Use a ham slice in place of cheese slice.

- Find out the differences between chimpanzees and gorillas.

- Visit a zoo to see different types of monkeys.

LEFTOVERS:

Mini stuffed mushrooms or tomatoes: For mushrooms, cut off stems and scoop out insides. Mix finely chopped stems and insides with a few bread crumbs, a little grated cheese, and a few chopped black olives. Stuff mushroom caps with bread crumb mixture. For tomatoes, cut off tops and scoop out tomato pulp. Mix pulp with a few bread crumbs, a little grated cheese, and a few chopped black olives. Stuff tomatoes with bread crumb mixture. Drizzle a little butter over tops of both mushrooms and tomatoes. Put on foil or broiler pan and broil a few minutes until tops are lightly browned.

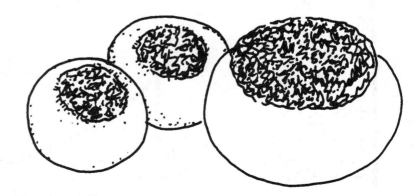

Mouse

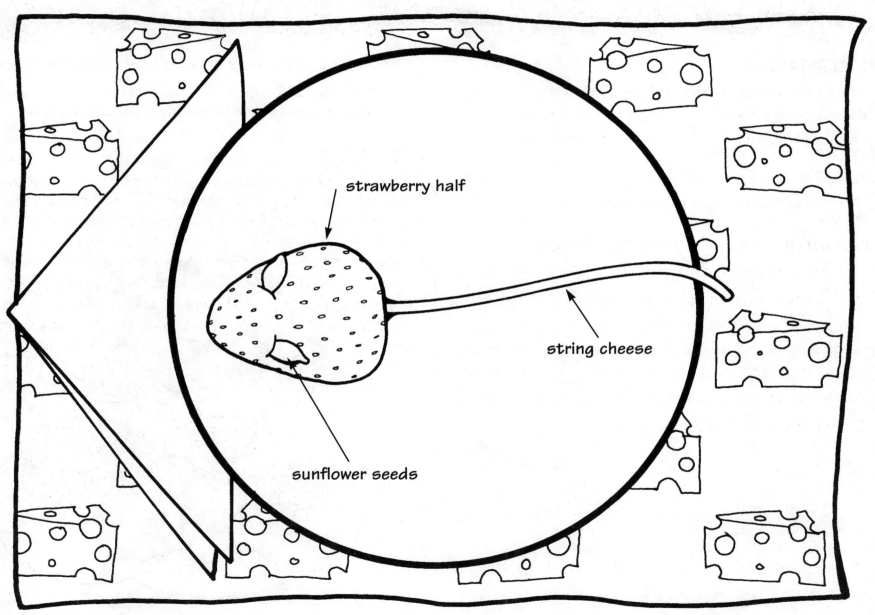

strawberry half

string cheese

sunflower seeds

Creating the Snack Art

INGREDIENTS

- one strawberry
- string cheese
- two sunflower seeds

UTENSILS

- cutting board
- paring knife

LET'S DO IT!

1. Cut strawberry in half and place one half cut side down.
2. Separate string cheese to make a tail.
3. Assemble ingredients as shown.

MORE IDEAS

- Make a stand-up mouse by cutting a whole strawberry flat at the stem end. Stand up on plate. Add ears and put tail under strawberry.
- Make mouse finger puppets by drawing mouse faces on fingers with washable markers.

LEFTOVERS

Ice cream and strawberries: Have ice cream topped with strawberries. Sprinkle with sunflower seeds, if desired.

88

Opossum

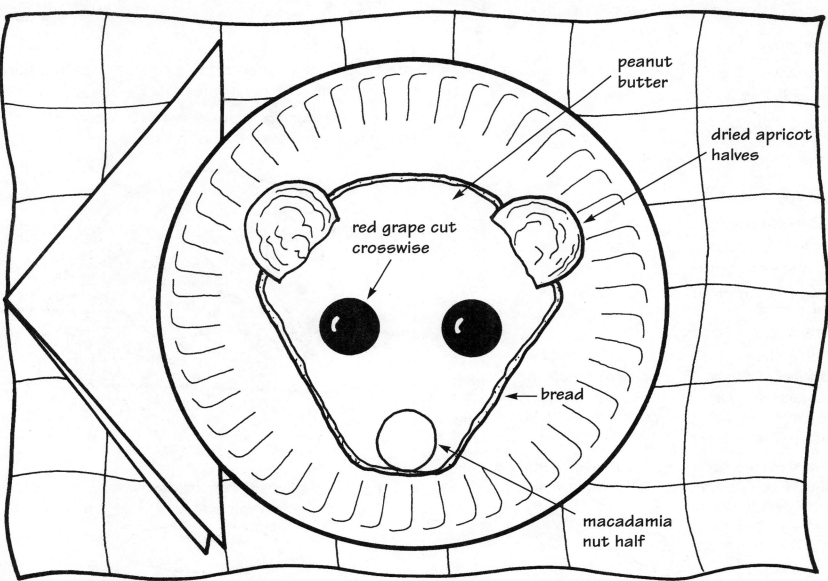

peanut butter

dried apricot halves

red grape cut crosswise

bread

macadamia nut half

#2318 Snack Art

Creating the Snack Art

INGREDIENTS

- bread slice
- one dried apricot
- two red grapes
- one macadamia nut

UTENSILS

- cutting board
- round drinking glass, about 3" in diameter
- paring knife
- table knife

LET'S DO IT!

1. Cut bread into a circle, using the glass as a guide. Cut small strips from both sides of the bread round to make the face more possum-like. Spread bread with peanut butter.

2. Cut dried apricot in two crosswise to make ears. Cut ends off grapes to use as eyes. Slice macadamia nut in half for nose.

3. Assemble remaining ingredients as shown.

MORE IDEAS

- Use small round cereal instead of macadamia nuts for the nose.

- Find out more about opossums. Where do they live? What do they eat?

LEFTOVERS

<u>Great snacks:</u> Dried apricots, grapes, and macadamia nuts make great snacks all by themselves.

Ostrich

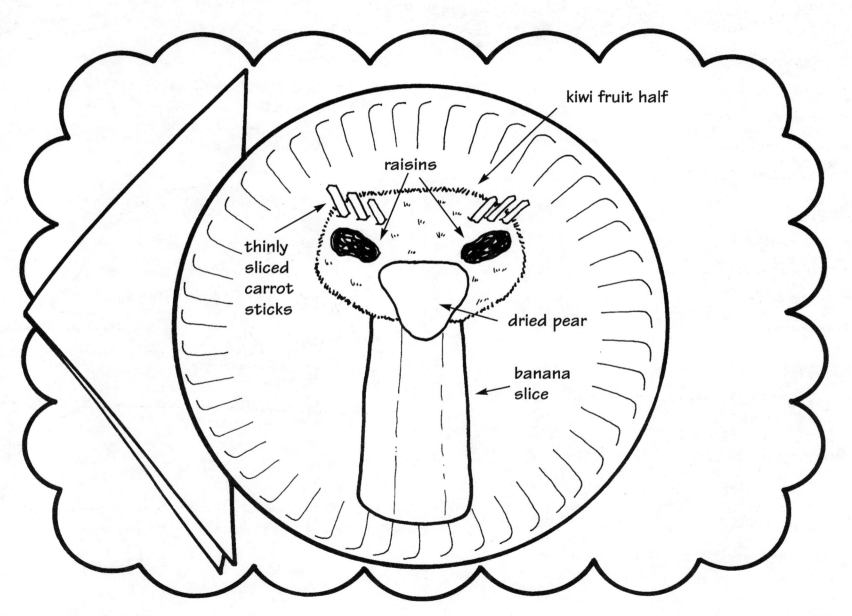

kiwi fruit half

raisins

thinly
sliced
carrot
sticks

dried pear

banana
slice

#2318 Snack Art

Creating the Snack Art

INGREDIENTS

- one kiwi fruit
- peanut butter or cream cheese
- two raisins
- carrot match sticks
- one dried pair
- one banana

UTENSILS

- cutting board
- paring knife

Note: This recipe requires fine motor skills and experience. Prepare ingredients ahead of time, if needed. (See page 7.)

LET'S DO IT!

1. Cut kiwi fruit in half lengthwise.
2. Use cream cheese or peanut butter as glue to attach raisins as eyes. Attach carrot eyelashes by inserting them directly into the kiwi fruit.
3. To make the neck, peel banana and slice in two lengthwise. From one half, cut a 2–3"-long piece.
4. Use dried pear as beak.
5. Assemble as shown.

MORE IDEAS

- For an easier version, remove crusts and cut an oval shape from a piece of bread. Spread bread with peanut butter, then arrange other ingredients to resemble ostrich face.
- Peel kiwi fruit before eating it.
- Have a fruit-tasting activity. Try other fruits that may be unfamiliar like mangos, papayas, boysenberries, or raspberries.
- Find out how much ostriches weigh. Compare that with the weight of a local bird.

LEFTOVERS

<u>Banana kiwi fruitsicles:</u> Mash one banana in a bowl; stir in ¼ cup chopped kiwi fruit (or use other fruits). Spoon mixture into a frozen pop mold or small plastic cup. Place frozen pop sticks or plastic spoons in the center of each cup. Freeze. Peel off cups before eating.

Otter

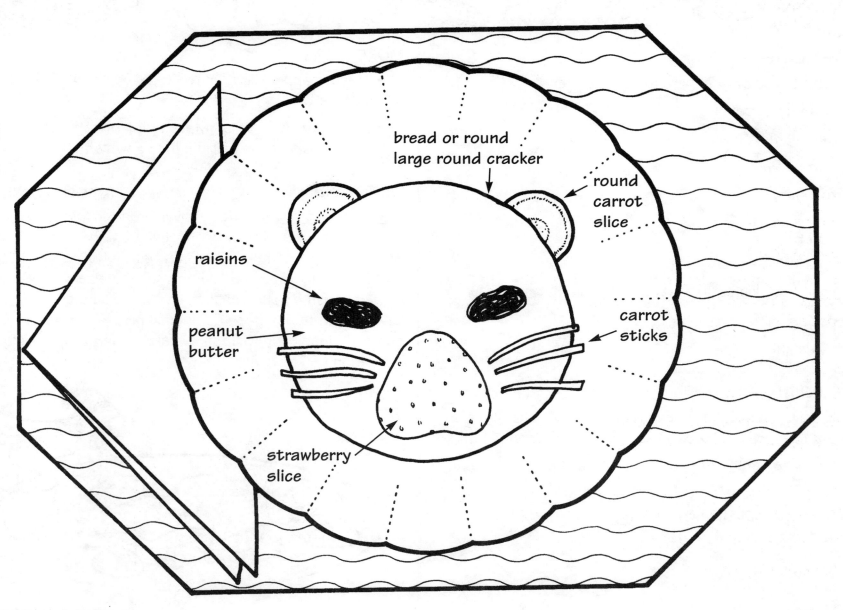

bread or round
large round cracker

round
carrot
slice

raisins

peanut
butter

carrot
sticks

strawberry
slice

Creating the Snack Art

INGREDIENTS

- bread slice or one large, round cracker
- peanut butter
- carrot match sticks
- two raisins
- one strawberry

UTENSILS

- cutting board
- round drinking glass, about 2" in diameter
- paring knife
- table knife

LET'S DO IT!

1. If using bread, cut it into a circle, using the glass as a guide. Spread bread or cracker with peanut butter.

2. For ears, cut a carrot slice in two; use half for each ear.

3. For nose, cut strawberry lengthwise and use an outside slice.

MORE IDEAS

- Use an apple slice for the head instead of bread or crackers.

- Learn about otters. Make a list of other animals that spend a lot of time in the water.

LEFTOVERS

French toast bites: Cut leftover bread into bite-size pieces. Dip bread in bowl containing one beaten egg mixed with $\frac{1}{4}$ cup milk. Then put it in a hot frying pan with a little melted margarine. When the bite-size pieces are golden brown on the bottom, use a spatula to turn several pieces at once. Cook until pieces are golden brown on both sides. Top with strawberries and a sprinkling of cinnamon.

Owl

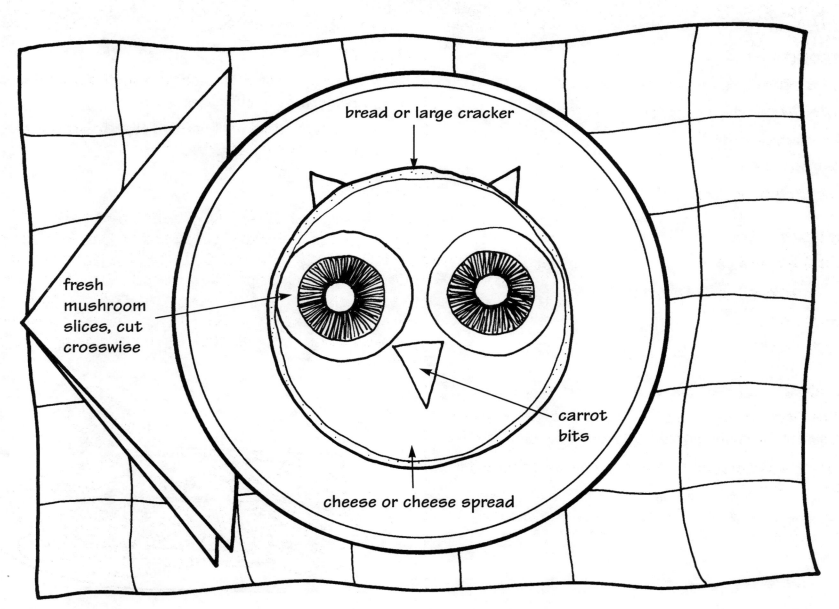

bread or large cracker

fresh mushroom slices, cut crosswise

carrot bits

cheese or cheese spread

Creating the Snack Art

INGREDIENTS

- bread slice or large, round cracker
- one slice of cheese, or cheese spread
- one carrot
- one mushroom

UTENSILS

- cutting board
- round drinking glass, about 3" in diameter
- paring knife
- table knife

LET'S DO IT!

1. If using bread, cut it into a circle, using the glass as a guide.
2. Slice mushrooms crosswise to use as eyes.
3. Cut carrot into bits to use as ears and beak.
2. Assemble ingredients as shown.

MORE IDEAS

- Use a piece of cheese cut in a circle to fit the bread in place of the cheese spread.
- Find out if owls really are wiser than other birds.
- Try to hoot like an owl.

LEFTOVERS

<u>Chicken and stuffing:</u> Preheat oven to 350°. Saute 2 tablespoons chopped onion, $\frac{1}{4}$ cup sliced mushrooms, and 1 tablespoon grated carrots in 2 tablespoons melted butter. Mix in bowl with 4 cups of bread crumbs and $\frac{1}{4}$ to $\frac{1}{2}$ cup chicken broth or water. Put in baking pan; cover with skinless, boneless chicken thighs. Lightly brush tops of chicken thighs with melted butter. Bake for 1 hour.

Panda

small prunes or prune halves

cream cheese

bagel half

red grape halves

large prune

raisins

Creating the Snack Art

INGREDIENTS

- bagel half
- cream cheese
- three small or two large prunes
- one red grape
- raisins

UTENSILS

- cutting board
- paring knife

LET'S DO IT!

1. Spread bagel with cream cheese.

2. For panda's mask, use one large prune thinly sliced through center to make two flat round pieces, or use two small prunes. Cut out center of prunes and add grape slices for eyes.

3. Assemble remaining ingredients as shown.

MORE IDEAS

- For a "sweet panda", use crumbled chocolate wafers instead of prunes for the mask.

- Pandas live in China and eat bamboo. Make a Chinese dish of canned bamboo shoots, sliced cooked chicken, and a little soy sauce.

- Pandas are an endangered species. Discuss what "endangered" means.

LEFTOVERS

More animals: Check index under "prunes" for other animal snack art recipes that call for prunes.

Pig

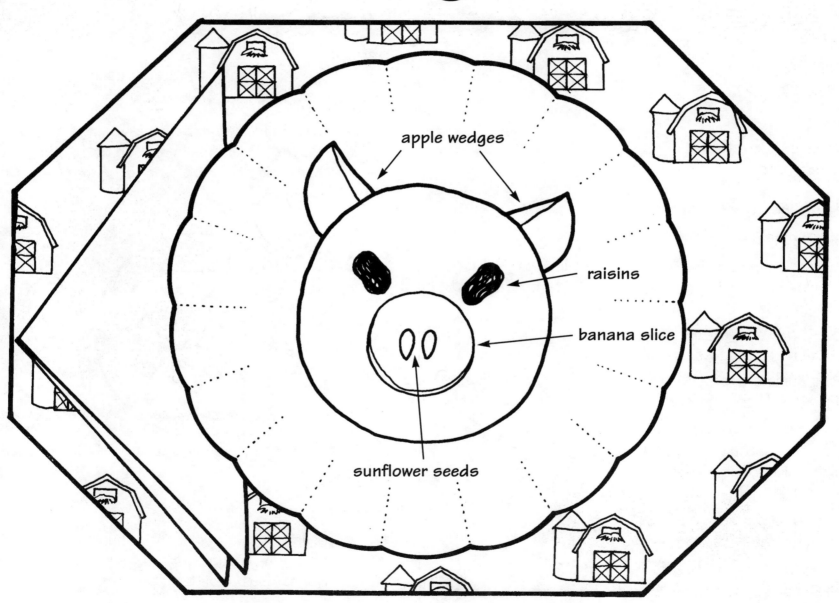

apple wedges

raisins

banana slice

sunflower seeds

Creating the Snack Art

INGREDIENTS

- one apple
- raisins
- one banana
- sunflower seeds

UTENSILS

- cutting board
- large knife to cut apple
- paring knife

Note: This recipe requires fine motor skills and experience. Prepare ingredients ahead of time, if needed. (See page 7.)

LET'S DO IT!

1. Cut apple crosswise into ¼" slices; remove seeds.

2. Top apple slice with ¼" thick slice of banana to create a snout.

3. Add raisins for eyes and sunflower seeds for nostrils, assembling the pig as shown.

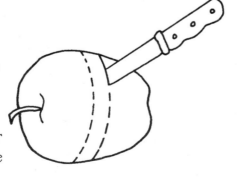

MORE IDEAS

- Sprinkle lemon juice on apple slices to prevent them from turning brown.

- Make paper plate pig masks. Draw pig faces on paper plates. Poke small holes on both sides of plate. Attach elastic string or cord to tie mask on. Cut holes for eyes.

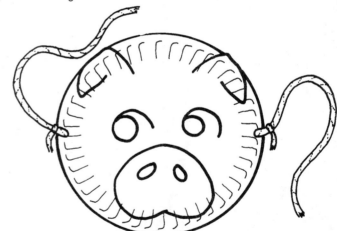

- Use masks to act out the story of "The Three Little Pigs."

LEFTOVER

<u>Waldorf salad:</u> Cut two apples into chunks. Add ¼ cup chopped dates and ¼ cup chopped walnuts. Stir in just enough mayonnaise to moisten (1–2 tablespoons).

Porcupine

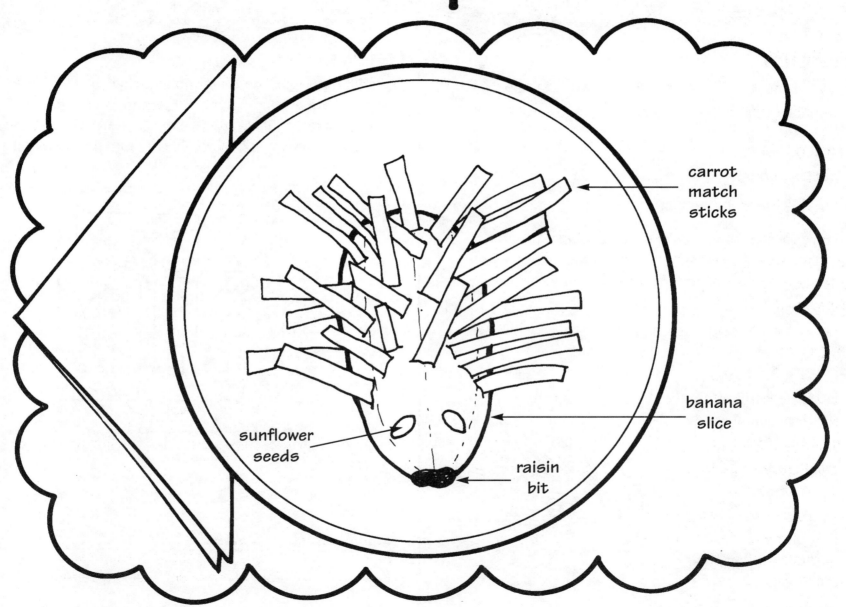

carrot
match
sticks

banana
slice

sunflower
seeds

raisin
bit

#2318 Snack Art

Creating the Snack Art

INGREDIENTS

- one banana
- sunflower seeds
- carrot match sticks
- one raisin

UTENSILS

- cutting board
- paring knife

LET'S DO IT!

1. To make the body, peel banana and cut crosswise 2" from an end. Cut this piece in two lengthwise; use one quarter piece for the body.

2. Stick the carrot match sticks, sunflower seeds, and raisin bit directly into the banana body as shown.

MORE IDEAS

- Sprinkle banana and carrots with a little lemon juice before assembling to prevent browning.

- Use canned pear half for body instead of banana.

- Find out how porcupines use their quills.

LEFTOVERS

Baked bananas: Slice bananas lengthwise into two pieces. Place in baking pan. For each banana, sprinkle on $\frac{1}{2}$ teaspoon lemon juice, $\frac{1}{2}$ teaspoon sugar, and $\frac{1}{4}$ teaspoon cinnamon. Bake at 350° for 15–20 minutes or until soft.

Rabbit

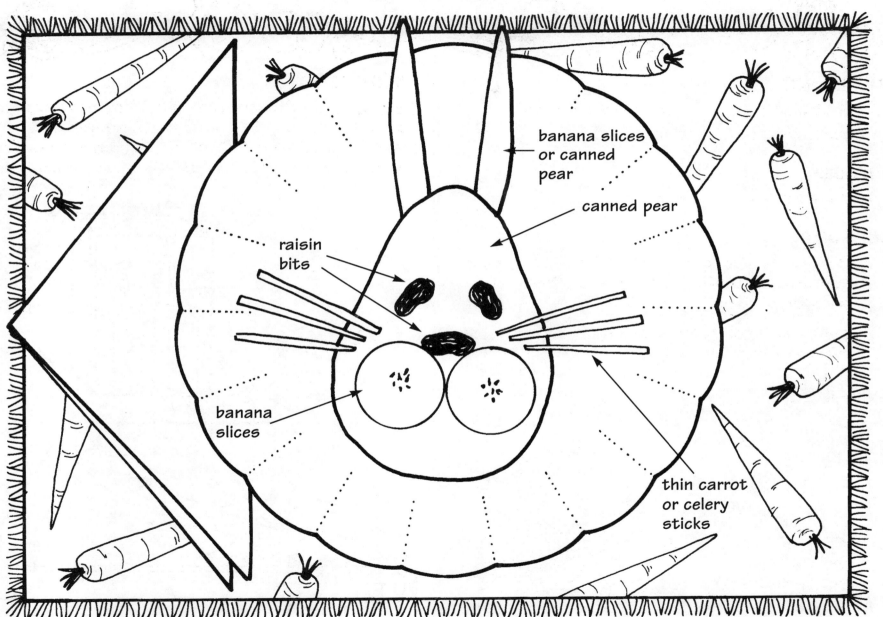

banana slices
or canned
pear

canned pear

raisin
bits

banana
slices

thin carrot
or celery
sticks

Creating the Snack Art

INGREDIENTS

- one canned pear
- one banana or additional canned pear
- raisin bits
- carrot or celery match sticks

UTENSILS

- cutting board
- paring knife

LET'S DO IT!

1. Place canned pear hollow-side down.
2. Cut ears from narrow end of second canned pear or a banana slice.
3. Assemble remaining ingredients as shown.

MORE IDEAS

- Plan a menu that might be shared with a rabbit. Some suggestions are lettuce, carrot sticks, and raw spinach.

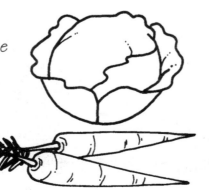

LEFTOVERS

Fruit salad: Cut any combination of fruits into chunks. Pour orange juice a little at a time over fruits until salad is just moistened. Serve cold.

Raccoon

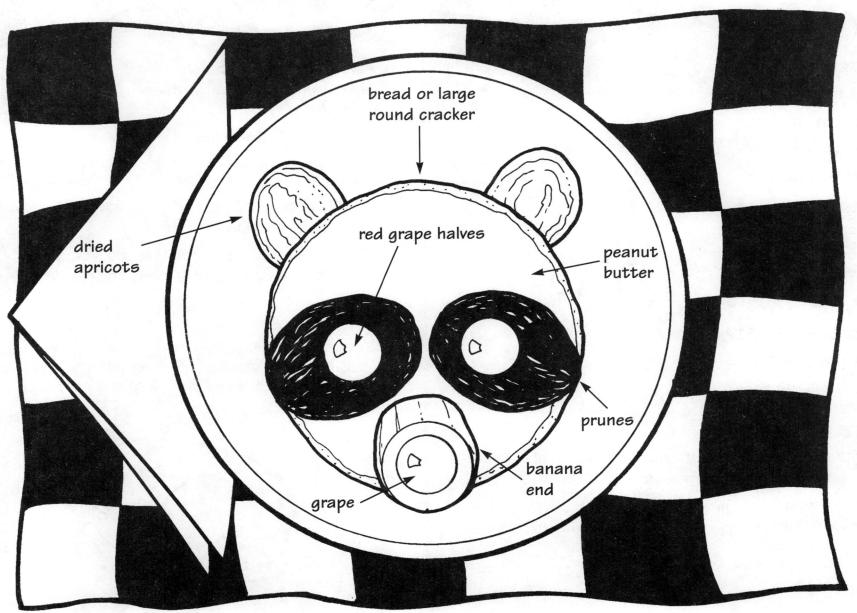

bread or large
round cracker

red grape halves

dried
apricots

peanut
butter

prunes

grape

banana
end

Creating the Snack Art

INGREDIENTS

- bread slice or large round cracker
- peanut butter
- two dried apricots
- one prune
- two red grapes
- one banana

UTENSILS

- cutting board
- round drinking glass, about 3" in diameter
- paring knife
- table knife

LET'S DO IT!

1. If using bread, cut into a circle, using a glass as a guide; spread bread or cracker with peanut butter.

2. For mask, slice prune thinly through center to make two round flat pieces. Add halved grapes as eyes.

3. Place banana and grape nose cut-side down on the peanut butter so that it appears to jut out from the face.

4. Assemble remaining ingredients as shown.

MORE IDEAS

- For a "sweet raccoon," use chocolate wafers instead of prunes for the mask.

- Raccoons are scavengers. Make up a story about raccoons eating leftovers, then eat some leftovers yourself.

LEFTOVERS

Addition to banana bread: Find a recipe for banana nut bread. Add ½ cup chopped prunes to the batter, then bake as directed.

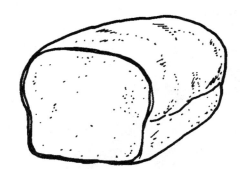

Rat

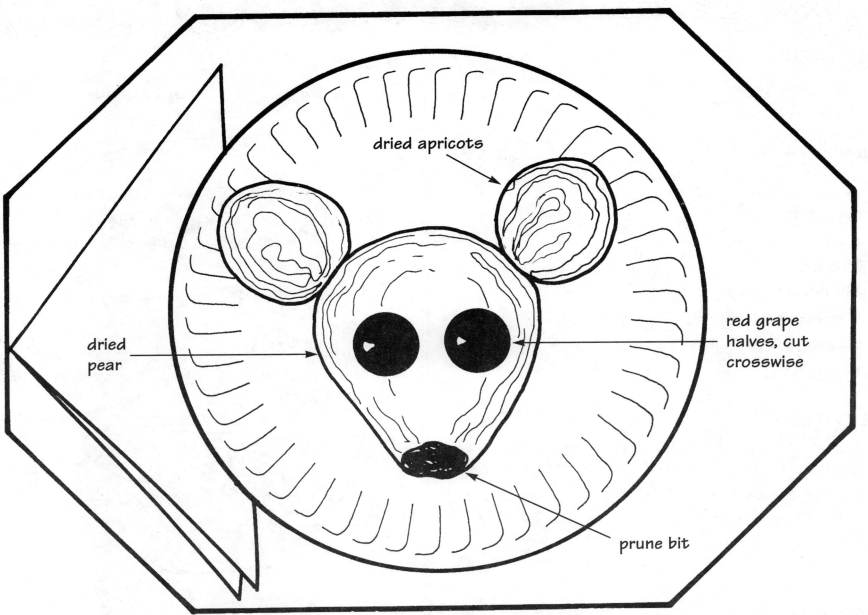

dried apricots

dried pear

red grape halves, cut crosswise

prune bit

#2318 Snack Art

Creating the Snack Art

INGREDIENTS

- one dried pear
- one red grape
- two dried apricots
- one raisin

UTENSILS

- cutting board
- paring knife

LET'S DO IT!

Assemble rat as shown.

MORE IDEAS

- Substitute prune bits for raisins to make nose.
- Discuss the intelligence of domestic rats.
- Explain the difference between domestic and wild rats. Discuss hygiene and why we don't share our food with wild rats.

LEFTOVERS

<u>Dried fruit and nut mix:</u> Chop up dried fruits. Mix with nuts and seeds. Keep in a tightly-closed plastic bag.

Rattlesnake

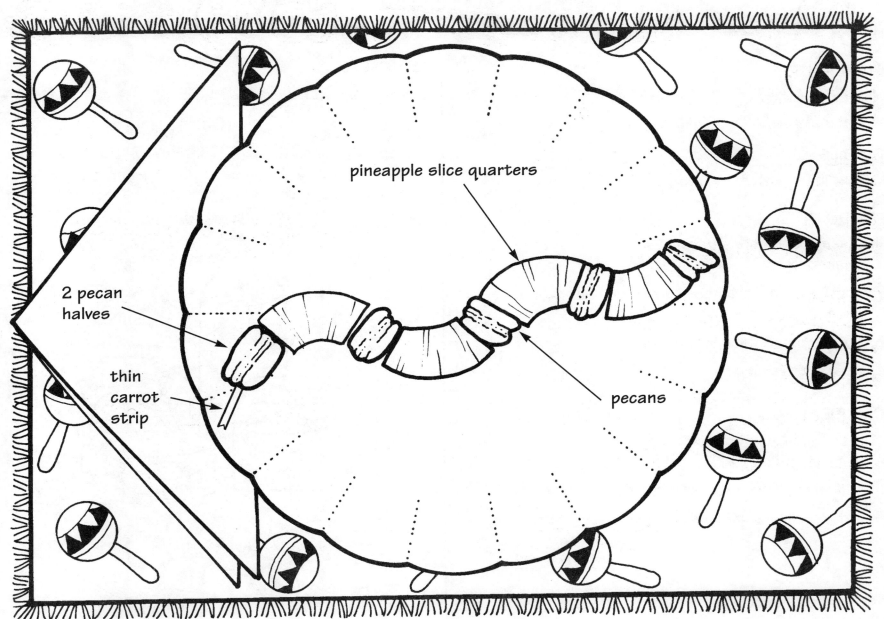

pineapple slice quarters

2 pecan halves

thin carrot strip

pecans

109

Creating the Snack Art

INGREDIENTS

- pecan halves
- one pineapple slice
- thin carrot strip

UTENSILS

- cutting board
- paring knife

LET'S DO IT!

1. Place pecan halves back to back to create the snake's head.

2. For tongue, insert carrot between back-to-back pecan halves.

3. Cut pineapple slice into quarters for body and rattle.

4. Assemble remaining ingredients as shown.

MORE IDEAS

- Use walnuts instead of pecans.

- Make cracker and fruit snakes: Alternate small rectangular crackers with cut pieces of fruits.

- Did you know some snakes can eat an entire mouse whole? Make strawberry mice to go with the snake.

LEFTOVERS

Gelatin with pineapple and nuts: Make a gelatin dessert mix. Add pineapple chunks and grated carrots, according to instructions on package. Add whipped topping and sprinkle with chopped pecans if desired. (Be sure to use canned pineapple! If you use fresh pineapple, the gelatin won't set.) Save the leftover pineapple juice. Pour into a glass and add ice for a nice cold drink.

Seal

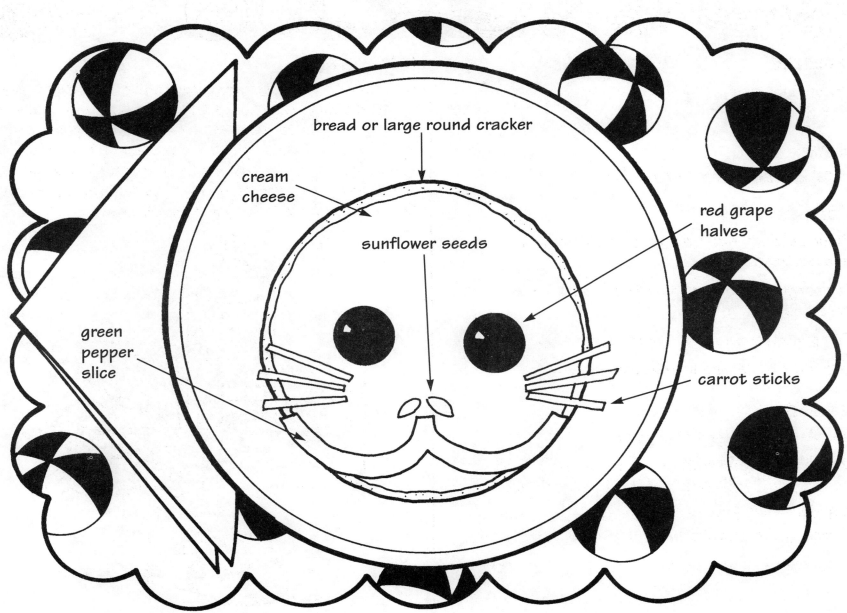

bread or large round cracker

cream cheese

sunflower seeds

red grape halves

green pepper slice

carrot sticks

#2318 Snack Art

Creating Snack Art

INGREDIENTS

- bread slice or large round cracker
- cream cheese
- one red grape
- sunflower seeds
- one green pepper slice
- carrot match sticks

UTENSILS

- cutting board
- round drinking glass, about 3" in diameter
- paring knife
- table knife

LET'S DO IT!

1. If using bread, cut it into a circle, using the glass as a guide. Spread bread or cracker with cream cheese.

2. Slice grape in half for eyes.

3. Use one thin slice of green pepper for muzzle.

4. Assemble ingredients as shown.

MORE IDEAS

- Find out where seals live and what they eat.
- Discuss why baby seals are white, while their parents are grey or black in color.

LEFTOVERS

Croutons on salad: Cut leftover bread into cubes and toast in oven until crisp, stirring occasionally. Use as croutons on top of a salad made from lettuce, green pepper slices, and shredded carrots.

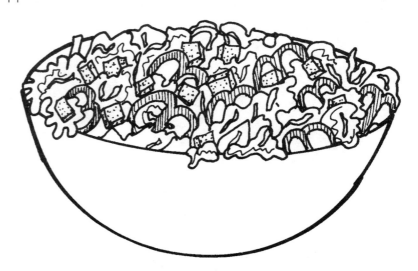

Turtle

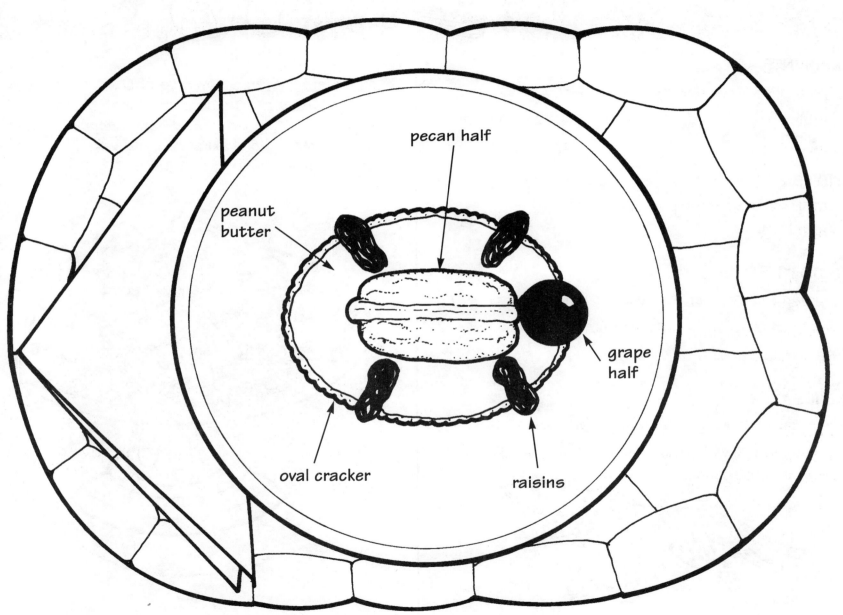

peanut butter

pecan half

grape half

oval cracker

raisins

#2318 Snack Art

Creating the Snack Art

INGREDIENTS

- one grape
- peanut butter
- raisins
- one oval cracker
- pecan half

UTENSILS

- cutting board
- table knife
- paring knife

LET'S DO IT!

1. Spread oval cracker with peanut butter.

2. Slice grape in half to create head.

3. Assemble ingredients as shown.

MORE IDEAS

- Use walnut halves instead of pecan halves.

- Turtles are slow-moving animals. Compare them to fast-moving animals.

LEFTOVERS

<u>Pecan squares:</u> Preheat oven to 350°. Stir together 1 egg and ³/₄ cup brown sugar. Stir in ¹/₂ cup flour and ¹/₄ teaspoon baking soda. Add 1 cup chopped pecans. Spread in greased 8" baking pan and bake for 19–20 minutes. Cut into squares to serve.

Snack Art for All Seasons

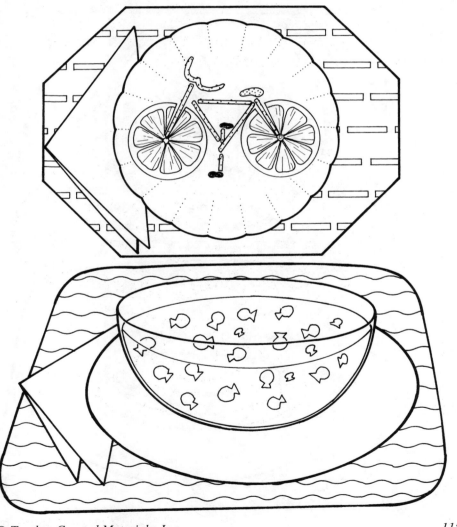

Snack Art for All Seasons *(cont.)*

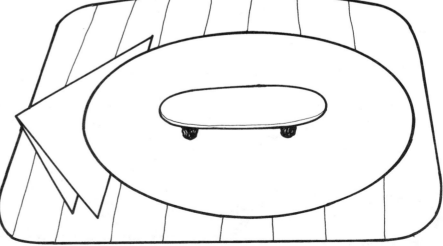

Football

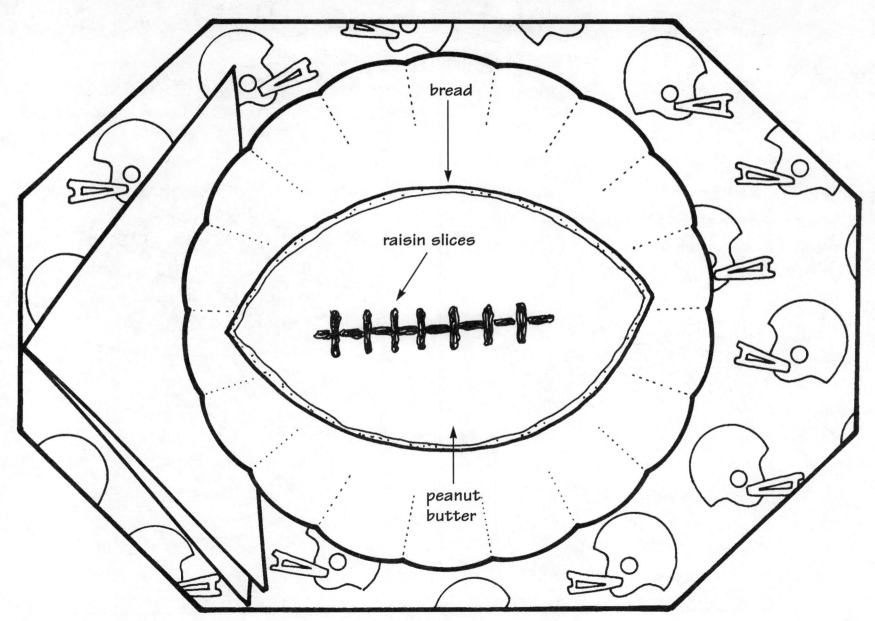

bread

raisin slices

peanut butter

#2318 Snack Art

Treating the Snack Art

INGREDIENTS

- bread slice
- peanut butter
- sliced raisins

UTENSILS

- cutting board
- paring knife
- table knife

LET'S DO IT!

1. Cut bread into the shape of a football.
2. Spread bread with peanut butter.
3. Add raisins as shown.

MORE IDEAS

- Toast bread footballs before adding peanut butter
- Make a football player.

LEFTOVERS

<u>Peanut butter coconut candy:</u> Combine 2 tablespoons peanut butter and ½ teaspoon frozen concentrated orange juice. Stir in 2 tablespoons shredded coconut. Roll into small balls.

Halloween Alien

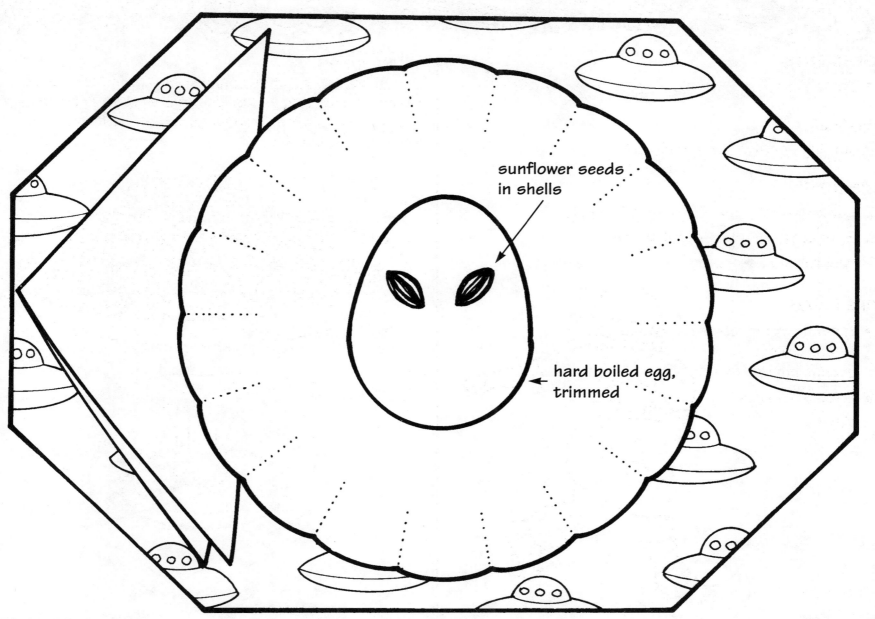

sunflower seeds
in shells

hard boiled egg,
trimmed

#2318 Snack Art

Creating the Snack Art

INGREDIENTS

- one hard boiled egg
- two sunflower seeds in shells

UTENSILS

- stove top
- cutting board
- sauce pan
- paring knife

LET'S DO IT!

1. Put cold egg in a saucepan with enough cold water to cover and heat to boiling. Reduce heat and simmer egg for six minutes; rinse in cold water.

2. When egg has cooled, remove shell and cut in two lengthwise; place each half yolk-side down on a plate.

3. With a paring knife, cut egg in the shape of an alien, as shown.

4. Push down lightly on sunflower seeds to stick them to egg.

MORE IDEAS

- Close your eyes and feel the "skin" of the alien, then open your eyes, turn the alien over and look at his yellow "brain"!

LEFTOVERS

Egg salad: Chop hard boiled egg and mix with mayonnaise to make egg salad for sandwiches or place salad on a lettuce leaf.

Thanksgiving Turkey

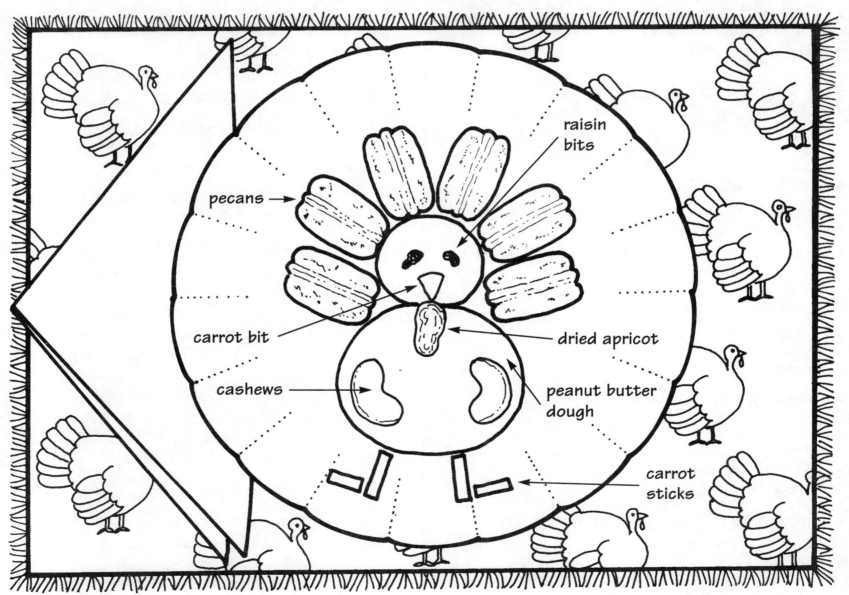

raisin bits

pecans

carrot bit

dried apricot

cashews

peanut butter dough

carrot sticks

#2318 Snack Art

Creating the Snack Art

INGREDIENTS

- peanut butter dough (see below)
- one carrot
- two raisins

- two cashews
- one dried apricot
- pecans
- two carrot sticks

PEANUT BUTTER DOUGH

- 1½ teaspoons concentrated orange juice

- 2 tablespoons peanut butter
- 1 tablespoon dried milk

UTENSILS

- cutting board
- paring knife

- bowl
- fork

LET'S DO IT!

Note: Make sure your hands are super clean for this recipe.

1. Make peanut butter dough: Stir concentrated orange juice into peanut butter. Add dried milk and form mixture into dough.

2. For body, make a 1½" ball from the dough; flatten slightly and place on plate.

3. For head, make a ½" ball from the dough; put on top of body, pushing it lightly to stick.

4. Attach carrot tip for beak, raisin bits for eyes, and cashews for wings.

5. Cut dried apricot waddle to fit; tuck under head.

6. Tuck pecan feathers and carrot legs under the body.

MORE IDEAS

- Use crackers spread with peanut butter instead of peanut butter dough for head and body.
- Use dough to make other animals or shapes.

LEFTOVERS

<u>Peanut butter muffins:</u> Preheat oven to 400°. In one bowl, mix together 1¾ cups all-purpose flour, ⅓ cup brown sugar and 2 teaspoons baking powder. In a separate bowl, mix 1 cup milk with ⅓ cup peanut butter (add milk a little at a time), 2 tablespoons vegetable oil, and 1 egg. Mix wet and dry ingredients together until just moistened. Fill greased baking cups ⅔ full. Bake 20 minutes or until golden brown.

Winter Reindeer

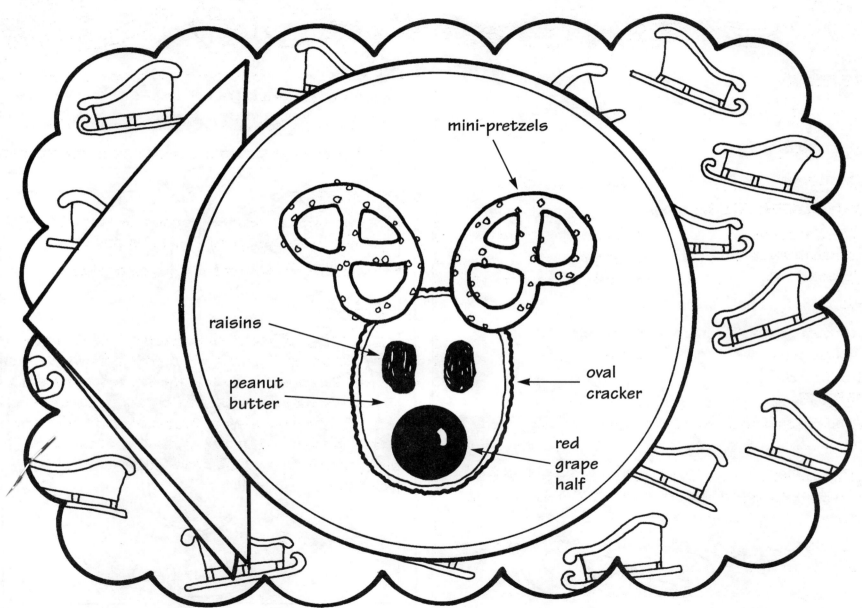

mini-pretzels

raisins

peanut
butter

oval
cracker

red
grape
half

Creating the Snack Art

INGREDIENTS

- one oval cracker
- one mini pretzel
- one red grape
- peanut butter
- two raisins

UTENSILS

- cutting board
- paring knife
- table knife

LET'S DO IT!

1. Spread cracker with peanut butter.

2. Cut grape in half for nose.

3. Arrange remaining ingredients as shown.

MORE IDEAS

- Use a maraschino cherry half instead of a grape for the nose.

- Make these reindeer as a holiday party activity. Put all the ingredients for the reindeer on a platter and let guests make their own.

LEFTOVERS

More reindeer: Make extra reindeer to take home as gifts. Provide small paper plates and plastic bags to transport them.

Snowman

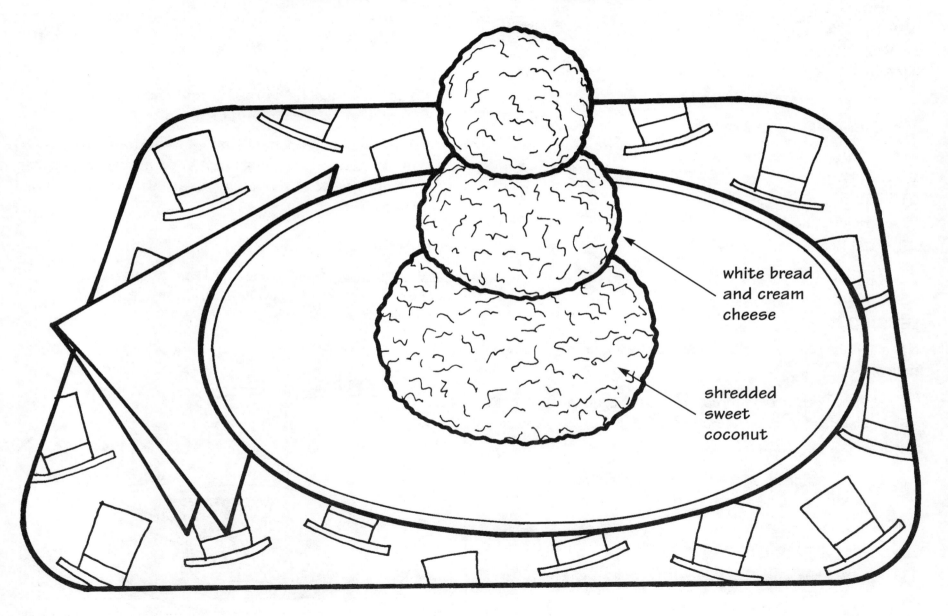

white bread
and cream
cheese

shredded
sweet
coconut

Creating the Snack Art

INGREDIENTS

- one slice white bread
- low-fat soft cream cheese
- shredded sweetened coconut

UTENSILS

- small mixing bowl
- fork
- spoon

LET'S DO IT!

Note: Make sure your hands are super clean for this recipe.

1. Remove crust from bread and tear crust or put it in a blender to make fine crumbs.

2. Soften 1 tablespoon cream cheese.

3. Mix together bread crumbs and cream cheese with a fork until dough starts to form.

4. Use hands to shape into large, medium, and small balls; roll balls in shredded coconut.

5. Pile the three balls as shown to make snowman.

MORE IDEAS

- Put on a face, using raisins and carrot bits. Add carrot-stick or mini-pretzel arms.

- Make flat snowmen by cutting white bread into 3 circles; arrange to look like a snowman. Spread with cream cheese if desired; decorate with cut fruits and vegetables.

LEFTOVERS

Toast squares: Toast bread and spread with cream cheese. Sprinkle with coconut, dried fruits, or nuts. Cut each slice into 4 squares.

Valentine's Day Muffin

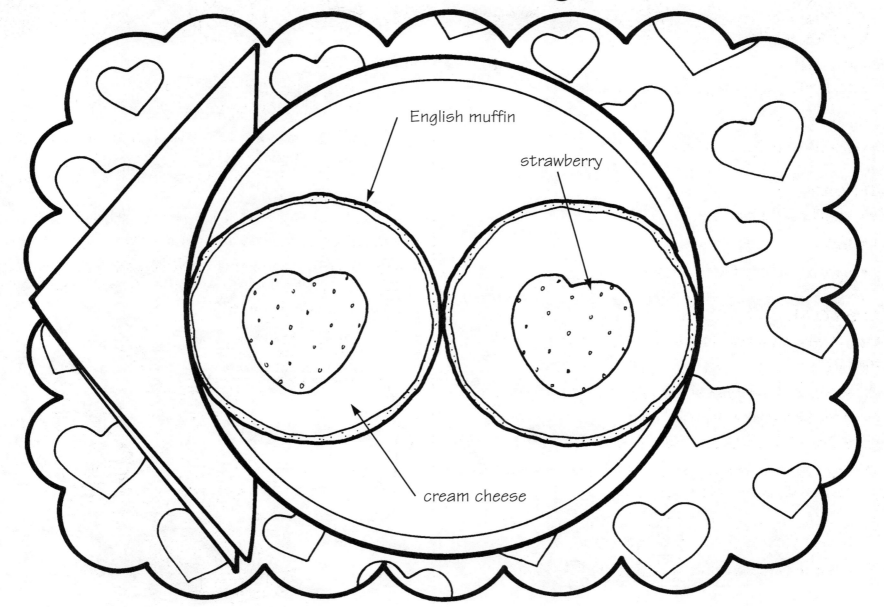

English muffin

strawberry

cream cheese

Creating the Snack Art

INGREDIENTS

- one English muffin
- one strawberry
- low-fat cream cheese

UTENSILS

- cutting board
- paring knife
- table knife

LET'S DO IT!

1. Split English muffin and toast.
2. Spread each half with cream cheese.
3. Cut strawberry in half lengthwise to make two heart shapes; put one on each muffin half.

MORE IDEAS

- Spell "I love you," using bits of dried fruit or nuts.
- Get up early and surprise someone special with a Valentine for breakfast.

LEFTOVERS

Try the following muffin meals.

Breakfast muffins: toast muffins; add cream cheese and jam.

Lunch muffins: toast muffins; mix cream cheese with finely chopped luncheon meat and spread on hot muffin.

Dinner muffins: make mini-pizzas by partially toasting muffins and topping with 1 tablespoon prepared pizza sauce and grated mozzarella cheese. Brown top under broiler until cheese melts.

Rainbow

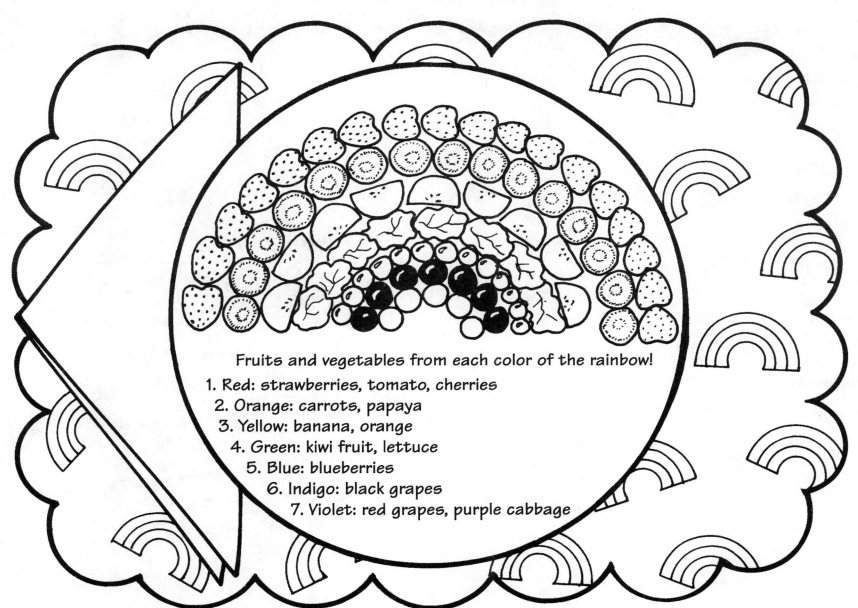

Fruits and vegetables from each color of the rainbow!

1. Red: strawberries, tomato, cherries
2. Orange: carrots, papaya
3. Yellow: banana, orange
4. Green: kiwi fruit, lettuce
5. Blue: blueberries
6. Indigo: black grapes
7. Violet: red grapes, purple cabbage

#2318 Snack Art

Creating the Snack Art

INGREDIENTS

- See page 129 for ideas.

UTENSILS

- cutting board
- paring knife
- chef's knife, if needed

LET'S DO IT!

1. Use small fruits or cut large fruits into bite-sized pieces.
2. Arrange fruits in curved lines to make a rainbow.

MORE IDEAS

- Make one enormous rainbow, using whole fruits.
- Indigo is a hard color to find. You can still make a nice rainbow without it.
- Take a trip to the grocery store just to look at all the beautiful colors in the produce department. Look for other fruits and vegetables to put in your rainbow.

LEFTOVERS

<u>Fruit pizza:</u> Make biscuits from a can or mix. Spread with low fat cream cheese. Top with a variety of chopped or sliced fruits.

Flowers

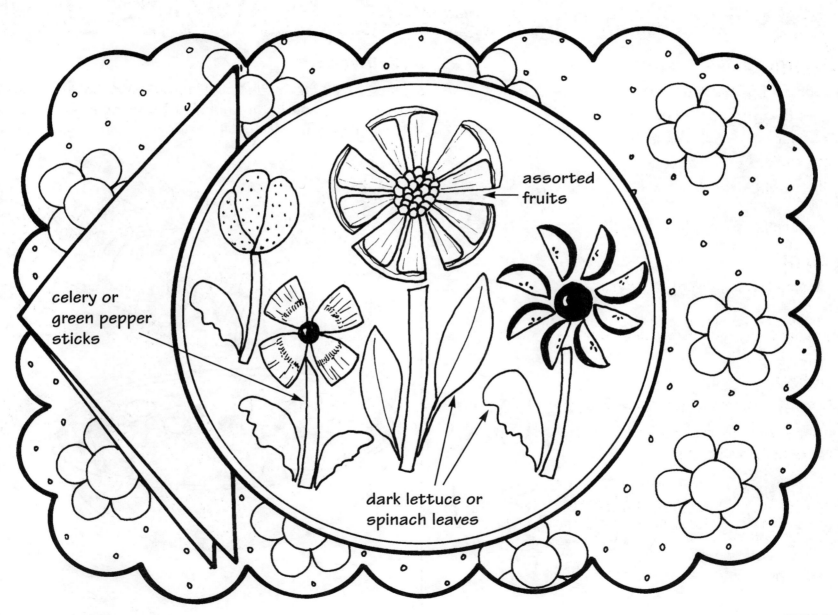

assorted fruits

celery or green pepper sticks

dark lettuce or spinach leaves

#2318 Snack Art

Creating the Snack Art

INGREDIENTS

- assorted fruits for petals
- celery or green pepper sticks
- dark lettuce or spinach leaves

UTENSILS

- cutting board
- paring knife
- chef's knife, if needed

LET'S DO IT!

1. Cut and arrange ingredients as shown.
2. Cut lettuce to size needed to make flower leaves.

MORE IDEAS

- Make a picture on a blue plate. Assemble alfalfa sprouts on the plate to look like grass. Add fruit flowers. Use a banana or apricot slice for the sun and little dots of yogurt for clouds.

LEFTOVERS

Lemon-lime fruit salad: Cut up an assortment of fruit into a bowl. Add just enough lemon-lime soda to coat fruit. Put in freezer until partially frozen. Eat ice cold.

Baseballs and Bats

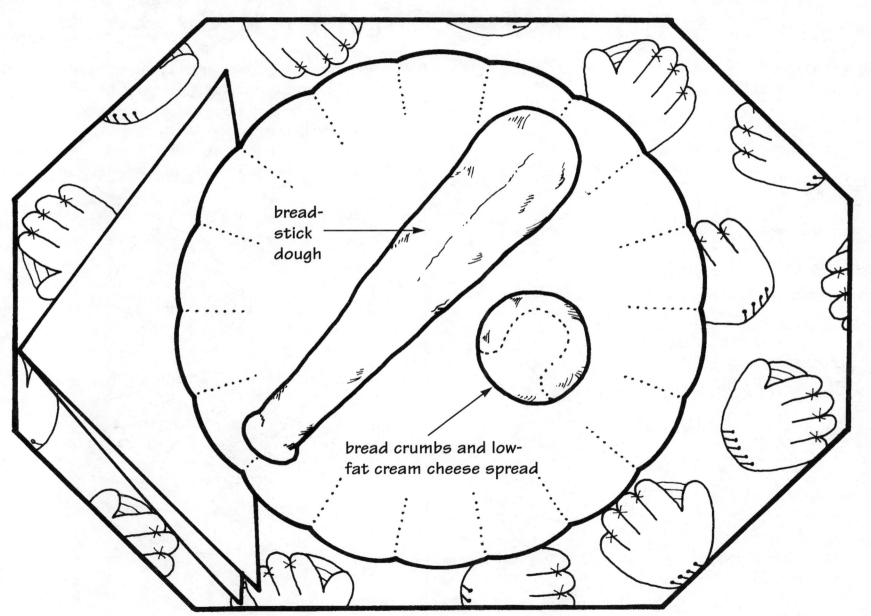

bread-stick dough

bread crumbs and low-fat cream cheese spread

#2318 Snack Art

Creating the Snack Art

INGREDIENTS

- bread slice
- low-fat cream cheese spread
- one can bread-stick dough

UTENSILS

- pan   • oven   • fork

LET'S DO IT!

Note: Make sure your hands are super clean for this recipe.

1. To make baseballs, Break bread into crumbs, and use a fork to mix them with 2 teaspoons of cream cheese to create a dough. Form dough into small balls. Use a toothpick or fork to poke holes in the "ball" to look like stitches.

2. To make bats, open can of bread-stick dough. Instead of twisting dough as directed, fold in two and form to look like a bat, pushing one end together to make it thicker and stretching the other end for the handle. Be sure to pinch seams where dough is folded. Bake dough, following package instructions.

MORE IDEAS

- To eat, flatten "baseball" and spread on "bat."

LEFTOVERS

Bread sticks: You can use remaining bread-stick dough to make bread sticks to eat with dinner.

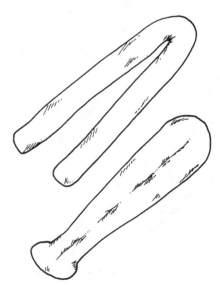

Bicycle

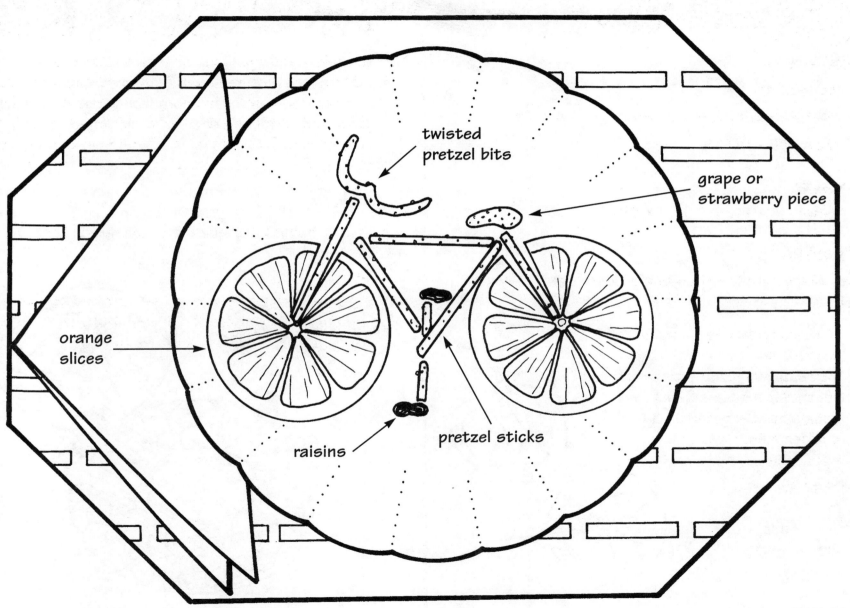

twisted
pretzel bits

grape or
strawberry piece

orange
slices

raisins

pretzel sticks

#2318 Snack Art

Creating the Snack Art

INGREDIENTS

- pretzel sticks
- one grape or strawberry
- two orange slices
- one twisted pretzel
- two raisins

UTENSILS

- cutting board
- paring knife

LET'S DO IT!

1. Arrange straight pretzel sticks to make bicycle frame, breaking pretzels as needed.

2. For handlebars, break twisted pretzel as shown; use curved part.

3. For seat, cut grape into quarters lengthwise; use one quarter. Or, if using strawberry, cut in a similar manner.

4. Cut two orange slices for the wheels. Make small cut to insert bike "frame" as shown.

5. Add raisins as pedals.

MORE IDEAS

- Add a piece of shredded or woven cereal as a basket, a round piece of cheese as a front light, and a piece of red grape, cherry, or dried cranberry as a reflector.

LEFTOVERS

Snack variety: Pretzels make great finger foods for a party. Serve with sliced vegetables and dip; add olives, chips, popcorn, and fruit juice for a complete variety of snacks.

Skateboard

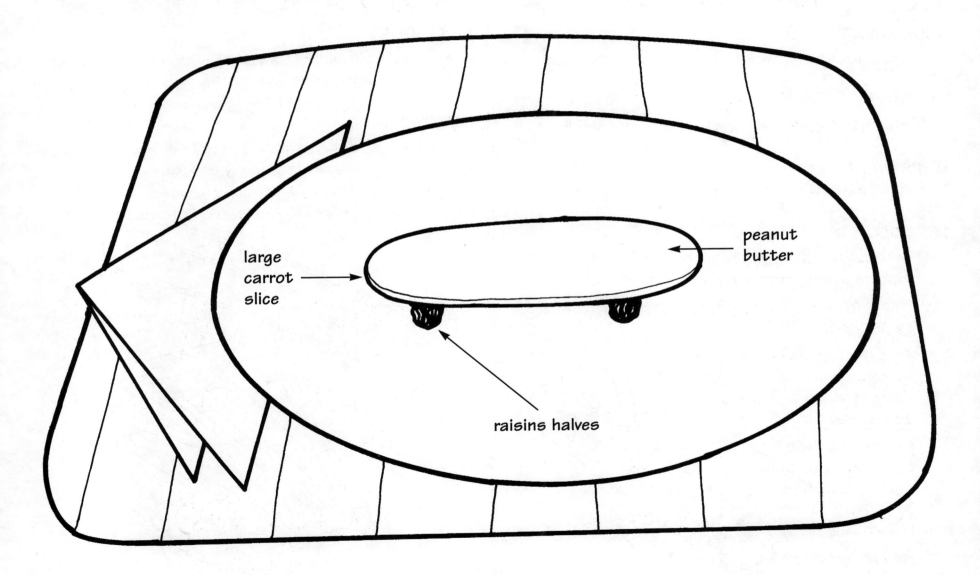

large
carrot
slice

peanut
butter

raisins halves

#2318 Snack Art

Creating the Snack Art

INGREDIENTS

- one carrot
- two raisins
- peanut butter

UTENSILS

- cutting board
- paring knife
- table knife

LET'S DO IT!

1. Cut the carrot into two- or three-inch chunks.

2. Slice the carrot chunk lengthwise into strips.

3. Trim ends of strips to make a rounded shape.

4. Spread peanut butter on bottom of carrot skateboard; glue on raisin halves as wheels and turn skateboard right side up.

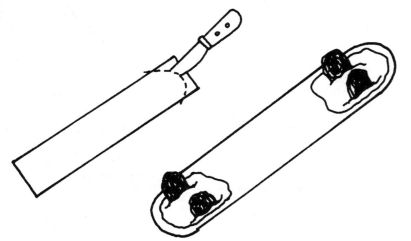

MORE IDEAS

- Using a toothpick, draw designs or stripes on top of skateboard with peanut butter.

LEFTOVERS

Carrot sticks: Cut carrots into sticks or slices. Keep in a bag in the refrigerator for easy snacks.

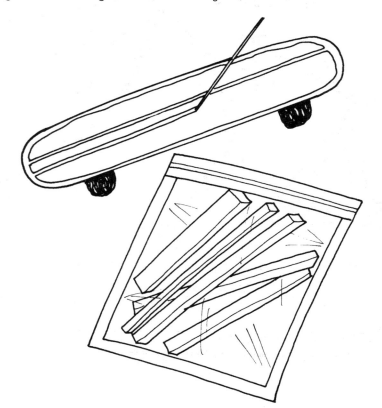

Fish in Water

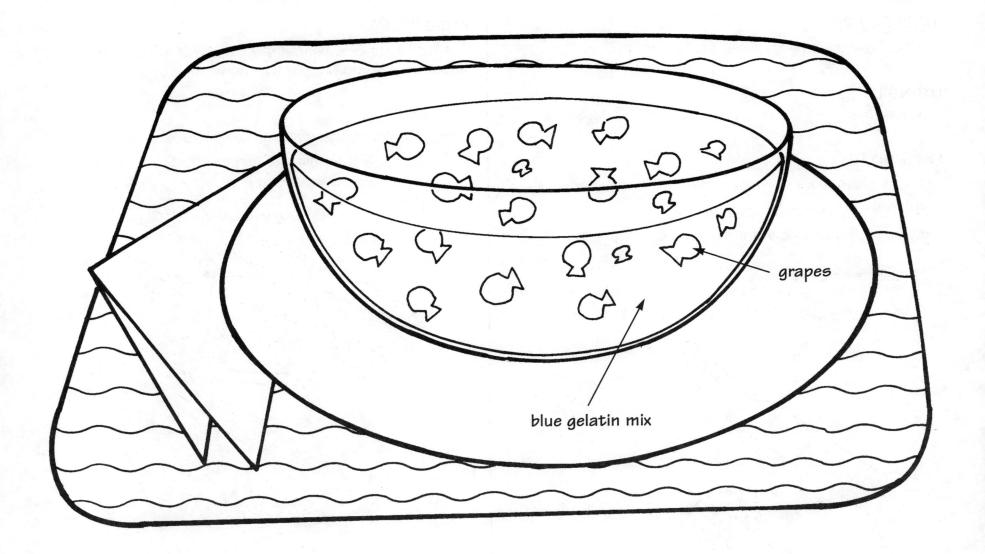

grapes

blue gelatin mix

#2318 Snack Art

Fish in Water

INGREDIENTS

- blue gelatin mix
- grapes

UTENSILS

- burner or stove top
- bowl
- spoon

LET'S DO IT!

1. Cut grapes in two lengthwise; cut into fish shape as shown.

2. Make gelatin according to package. When gelatin is just starting to set—approximately one hour after chilling—fold in grape "fish."

MORE IDEAS

- Make this recipe in a large glass bowl for a fish bowl effect or divide up mixture into individual cups or glasses before gelatin sets.

- Make fish appear to be in waves in the ocean: After gelatin has set, stir in 1 cup of low fat whipped topping. Let it set at least another hour before eating.

whipped cream

LEFTOVERS

No leftovers for this one. Eat it for lunch, snack, dinner or dessert.

Snack Art Nutrition Activities

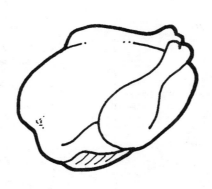

Snack Art Nutrition Activities *(cont.)*

Learning about food and nutrition can be fun. The following pages include activities and recipes that reinforce nutritious food choices, such as:

- A copy of the Food Pyramid.

- Let's Do It! for food-pyramid placemats and puzzle.

- Instructions and cards for playing "Go Eat," a food pyramid card game.

- Celebrating birthdays with a super cake.

- Going on a picnic with fun, healthy foods.

- Staying healthy with sports, using a "Feed Me" puppet.

- Having fun with science fiction by having "alien" snacks and baking "Moon Rock Cookies."

The Food Pyramid

The Food Guide Pyramid was created by the United States Department of Agriculture (USDA) as a way of presenting our government's latest guidelines for a healthy diet. The following pyramid shows what a daily balanced diet looks like.

A Guide to Daily Food Choices

Key

● Fat (naturally occurring and added)

▼ Sugars (naturally occurring and added)

These symbols show that fat and added sugars come mostly from fats, oils, and sweets, but can be part of or added to foods from the other food groups as well.

Fats, Oils, and Sweets
(Use sparingly.)

Milk, Yogurt, and Cheese Group

Meat, Poultry, Fish, Dry Beans, Eggs, and Nuts Group

2–3 Servings

2–3 Servings

Vegetable Group

Fruit Group

3–5 Servings

2–4 Servings

6–11 Servings

Bread, Cereal, Rice, and Pasta Group

#2318 Snack Art

The Food Pyramid (cont.)

SERVING SIZES

To help you determine the amount of food that makes up a serving size, the U.S. Department of Agriculture has established these guidelines.

BREAD, CEREAL, RICE & PASTA (STARCH)

- 1 slice bread
- 1 tortilla
- ½ cup cooked rice, pasta or cereal
- 1 ounce ready-to-eat cereal
- 3–4 small crackers

VEGETABLES

- ½ cup chopped raw or cooked vegetables
- 1 cup leafy raw vegetables

FRUITS

- 1 piece fruit or melon wedge
- ¾ cup fruit juice
- ½ cup cooked or canned fruit
- ¼ cup dried fruit

MILK, YOGURT & CHEESE (CALCIUM)

- 1 cup milk or yogurt
- 1½–2 ounces cheese
- 1½ cups ice cream or ice milk

MEAT, POULTRY, FISH, DRY BEANS, EGG & NUTS (PROTEIN)

- 2 ½ to 3 ounces cooked lean meat, poultry or fish
- Count ½ cup cooked beans, 1 egg, 1 tablespoon peanut butter, or ⅓ cup nuts as 1 ounce of meat

FATS, OILS & SWEETS

- Limit calories from these, especially if you want to lose weight.

The amount you eat may be more than one serving. For example, a dinner portion of spaghetti would count as two or three servings of pasta.

It is felt that grains and the foods made from them should be the foundation of our diet, providing about 40% of our total daily food intake, whereas fats and sweets should be used sparingly. Most nutrition experts agree that a diet rich in whole grains and complex carbohydrates provides us with the good health we need to lead active lives.

The Food Pyramid *(cont.)*

MAKE FOOD PYRAMID PLACEMATS

MATERIALS

- Food Pyramid on page 143
- colored markers, pencils or crayons
- laminating film

EQUIPMENT

- copy machine

LET'S DO IT!

- Make individual copies of page 143. Color or decorate as desired. Laminate on both sides to make reusable placemats.

MORE IDEAS:

- Cut out pictures of food from magazines and glue in the appropriate pyramid spaces before laminating.

- Before preparing a snack, put a laminated placemat in the middle of the table. Place pre-cut foods on top of matching food pyramid spaces.

- As an alternative, make placemats out of the food group cards found on pages 148–150.

#2318 Snack Art

The Food Pyramid *(cont.)*

FOOD PYRAMID PUZZLE

MATERIALS

- Food Pyramid on page 143
- dark pencil or marker

EQUIPMENT

- copy machine

LET'S DO IT!:

- Copy page 143 onto heavy paper. Cut into pieces along lines of pyramid or draw puzzle lines on the back of the paper and cut.

MORE IDEAS

- Cut along pyramid lines, then cut each of the blocks into smaller puzzle pieces. For a group of six children, have each group put together one large block, and then bring the blocks together to form the pyramid.

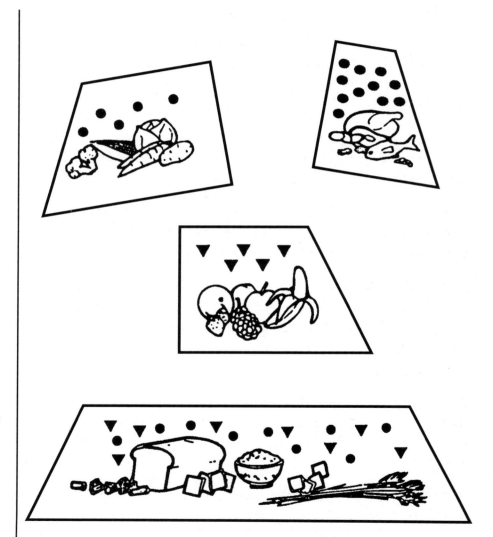

GO EAT

"Go Eat" is played in the same manner as the game "Go Fish," using the Food Pyramid as inspiration for the playing cards. The object of the game is to collect one card from each of the six food-pyramid food groups.

Prepare by copying one set of cards (see pages 148–150) for every two players onto heavy paper or card stock. Cut cards apart; color and laminate if desired.

To play, deal six cards to each child. Place remaining cards facedown in a stack in the center. Flip the top card over next to pile to begin a discard stack.

Player #1 may either pick up the card that is face up on the discard pile or ask any another player "Do you have any _____?" (fruits, vegetables, grains, protein foods, calcium foods or fats/sweet—whichever is needed to complete the pyramid).

If the player asked has the requested card, then he or she must give it to player #1. Player #1 then discards a card that is not needed face up on top of the discard pile.

If the player asked doesn't have the requested card, he or she says "Go eat!" Player #1 picks a card from the original stack and places an unwanted card on top of the discard pile.

Play around the circle clockwise. The first child to get all six food groups shows his or her cards and wins the game.

Note that after the first player finishes his or her first play, if there is more than one card in the discard pile, only the top card may be chosen by the players when told to "Go eat!"

MORE IDEAS

Use the cards to play matching games:

1. Give each child a card. Have them match with another child's card (fruit with fruit, starch with starch, etc.)

2. Spread all the cards out on the table. Have children try to form a pyramid by picking one food from each group.

3. Match the card to the pyramid. Give each child three or four cards. Ask them to show you where they fit on the pyramid. Give small prizes for correct answers.

The Food Pyramid (cont.)

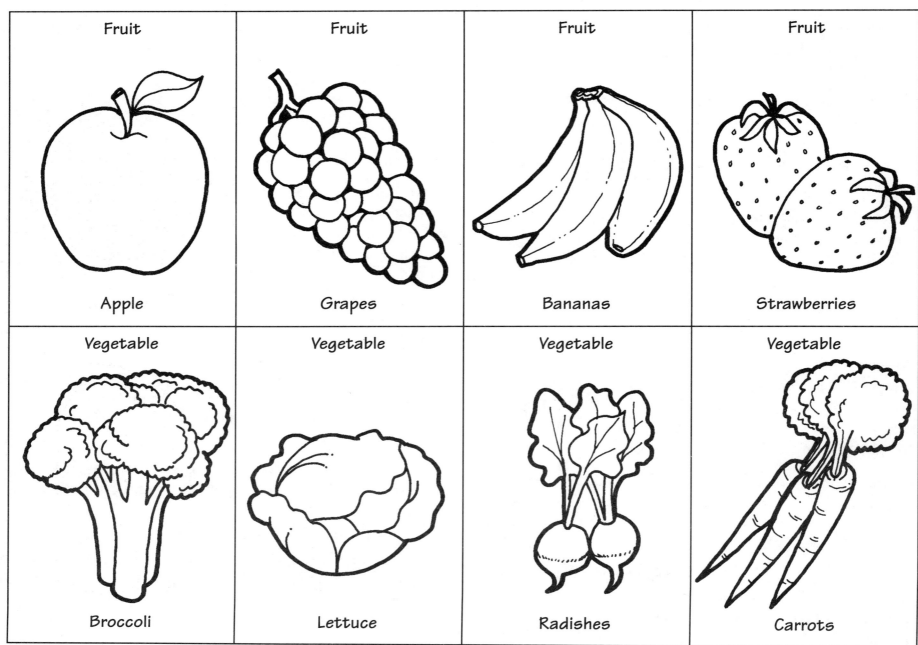

Fruit	Fruit	Fruit	Fruit
Apple	Grapes	Bananas	Strawberries

Vegetable	Vegetable	Vegetable	Vegetable
Broccoli	Lettuce	Radishes	Carrots

The Food Pyramid *(cont.)*

Starch	Starch	Starch	Starch
Bread	Rice	Potatoes	Noodles

Calcium	Calcium	Calcium	Calcium
Yogurt	Cheese	Peanuts	Milk

The Food Pyramid *(cont.)*

Protein	Protein	Protein	Protein
Beef	Chicken	Beans and Tofu	Fish

Fat	Fat	Sweets	Sweets
Oil	Butter	Cake	Candy

Celebrating Birthdays

BIRTHDAY CAKE WITH FRUIT

INGREDIENTS

- ¹/₃ cup margarine
- ¼ cup sugar
- 2 eggs
- 2 teaspoons vanilla
- 2 ¹/₃ cups flour
- ¹/₂ teaspoon baking soda
- ¼ teaspoon salt
- 1 teaspoon baking powder
- assorted fruit
- 1 cup nonfat yogurt
- 2 teaspoons grated orange peel

UTENSILS

- mixing bowl
- mixing spoon
- round cake pan
- cutting board
- paring knife

LET'S DO IT!

Preheat oven to 350°. Cream sugar and margarine with an electric mixer until light and fluffy. Add eggs and vanilla. Beat 3 minutes on medium. In a separate bowl, mix together dry ingredients, including orange peel. Stir dry ingredients into creamed mixture. Pour into greased and lightly-floured round cake pan. Bake for 60 minutes. Decorate with sliced fruits. (If you are using bananas, apples, or other fruits that turn brown, dip them in lemon juice before adding to the top of the cake.)

Celebrating Birthdays *(cont.)*

STICK THE FOOD ON THE FOOD PYRAMID

Play this spin-off of "Pin the Tail on the Donkey" at the birthday party to reinforce the Food Pyramid guidelines.

MATERIALS

- enlarged copy of the Food Pyramid (p. 143)
- pictures of food
- copies of food cards (p. 148–150; optional)
- tape or sticky putty
- material to make a blindfold

LET'S DO IT!

Enlarge a copy of the food pyramid. Attach tape or sticky putty to the back of the pictures and/or food cards. For younger children, direct the blindfolded player to stand about 3' from the poster, and provide a food picture or card for the player to attach to pyramid. Older children can be spun a few times before performing this task. After attaching the food picture, take off the blindfold and see if the player matched the food to the correct food group. If not, the player can place it where it should go. Provide healthy treats such as dried fruit bits, if desired.

Going on a Picnic

PEANUT BUTTER AND ANT SANDWICH

INGREDIENTS

- two slices bread
- peanut butter
- grapes

UTENSILS

- cutting board
- paring knife
- sandwich bags

LET'S DO IT!

Spread peanut butter on one piece of bread. Place grape ants (page 38) on peanut butter. Cover with another slice of bread.

MORE IDEAS

Take along some fruit juice in a cooler with ice. Don't forget paper or plastic cups and napkins.

#2318 Snack Art

SANDWICH TAG

Talk about all the good things that can be put on sandwiches. Let each child pick a sandwich ingredient (bread, peanut butter, tuna, cheese, lettuce, etc.) or pin a picture or name of a sandwich ingredient on each child. Form a circle.

"Bread" starts the game by walking around the outside of the circle and tapping another sandwich ingredient, for example "Lettuce". "Lettuce" chases "Bread," with "Bread" trying to get back to "Lettuce's" spot before being tagged.

Both "ingredients" go into the middle of the circle to build the "sandwich". Whichever "ingredient" makes it back to the original spot first picks another ingredients in the circle to start the game again.

Continue playing until the sandwich is complete (all ingredients have been chosen).

MORE IDEAS

- Make other kinds of sandwiches.

- **Caution:** If you make sandwiches from meats or other ingredients that are cold, be sure to keep them cold in a cooler until ready to eat.

- Take bread crumbs for the birds. Put little crumbs on the ground and follow the ants as they carry them away.

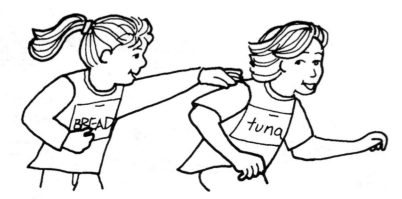

154

Stay Healthy With Sports

Prepare one of the sports-related snack art recipes from this book:

- football player (page 29)
- football (page 117)
- baseballs and bats (page 133)
- bicycle (page 135)
- skateboard (page 137)

Or create your own! Try thinking up a way to make a soccer ball, a pair of skates, or a hockey puck and stick.

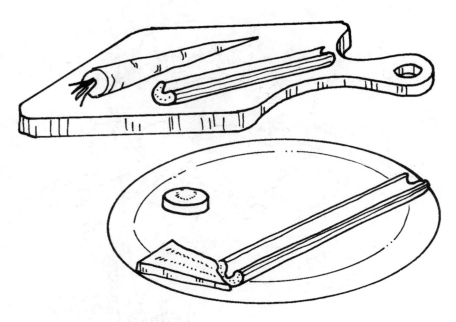

Peanut Butter

"FEED ME" PAPER BAG PUPPETS

MATERIALS

- small paper bag
- felt tip markers
- fabric or colored scrap paper
- scissors
- small pictures of nutritious foods (use magazines or clip art, or draw your own)
- string, yarn or rubber band

LET'S DO IT!

- Using the illustration as a guide, draw a face on the front of a small paper bag. If desired, include sports-related accessories (helmet for bicycling, shoulder pads for football, baseball cap for baseball, etc.) Cut a hole where the mouth is. Tie the bottom of the puppet around your wrist with string or yarn so that it stays on securely while you "feed" it.

- Feed puppets nutritious foods (pictures) to give them the energy needed to exercise and have fun.

MORE IDEAS

Do arm exercise with the puppets.

Make other kinds of puppets, like sock puppets or puppets from a book pattern.

Instead of individual puppets, make one big puppet face: With the open end up, draw a face on a large paper bag. Cut a hole for the mouth. Open the bag, then fold over the top. Take turns "feeding" the puppet pictures of nutritious foods.

MOON ROCK COOKIES

UTENSILS

- mixing bowl
- mixing spoon
- teaspoon
- cookie sheet
- measuring cups and spoons

RECIPE

- 1½ cups flour
- 1 teaspoon baking soda
- 1 cup applesauce
- 1 teaspoon cinnamon
- 1 cup brown sugar
- 2 eggs
- 1 teaspoon vanilla
- 3 cups rolled oats
- 1 cup raisins
- ½ cup chopped nuts

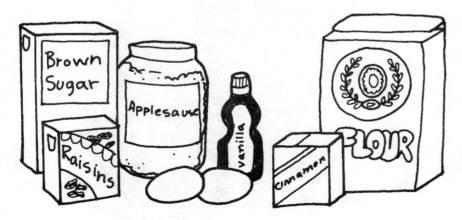

Preheat oven to 350°. Mix together flour, baking soda, and cinnamon in a bowl. Set aside. Cream together applesauce and brown sugar. Beat in eggs and vanilla. Add flour mixture, and mix well. Stir in oats, raisins, and nuts. Drop by rounded teaspoon onto lightly greased cookie sheet. Bake for 8 to 10 minutes or until golden brown. Makes about 4 dozen cookies.

Have Fun with Science Fiction *(cont.)*

MYSTERY LABEL GAME

Gather labels from a variety of foods. Cut off the list of ingredients and copy each list onto a separate card or sheet of paper. Try to guess which label matches which ingredients.

Good labels for younger children: bread, peanut butter, vegetable soup, fruit juice.

Good labels for older children: mayonnaise, crackers, cereals, pet food.

Try to find some foods with lots of scientific names to make it more challenging.

MORE IDEAS

- Make a spaceship from a refrigerator or other large box. Cut a door to get in and out.

- Plan a menu to take into space.

- Make aliens (page 119) as snacks, served alongside glasses filled with sports drinks in hot colors.

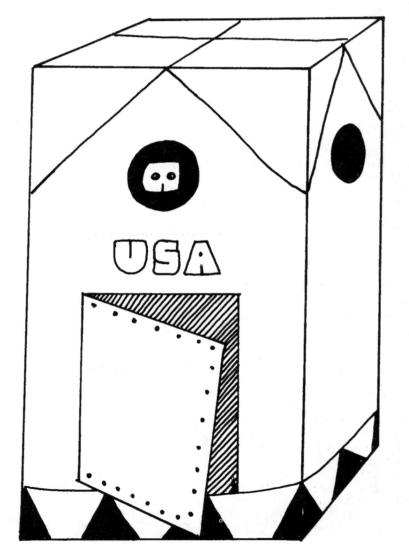

Ideas For Leftovers

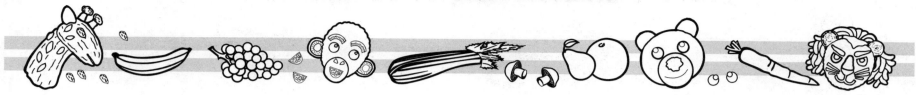

BREADS AND BUNS
bagel snacks (bear) 44
bread crumb coating for fish or chicken (koala bear) 78
broccoli topped with bread crumbs and grated cheese (lion) 84
checkerboard sandwiches (chef) 26
chili dogs with grated cheese (horse) 76
croutons on salad (seal) 112
French toast bites (otter) 94
jazzed up hamburgers (football player) 30
meat loaf (buffalo) 50
mini stuffed tomatoes or mushrooms (monkey) 86
muffin meals (Valentine) 128
rice crackers with toppings (Japanese doll) 32
stuffing (owl) 96
toast squares (snowman) 126
tuna patties (beaver) 46

CHEESE
broccoli topped with bread crumbs and grated cheese (lion) 84
chili dogs with grated cheese (horse) 76
cottage cheese fruit parfait (lamb) 80
mini stuffed tomatoes or mushrooms (monkey) 86
olive and cheese sandwiches (ant) 40

FRUITS
addition to banana nut bread (raccoon) 106
addition to homemade bread (leopard) 82
addition to muffins (fox) 66
baked bananas (porcupine) 102
bagels topped with cream cheese and chopped fruit (bear) 44
banana kiwi fruitsicle (ostrich) 92
banana milk (cow) 60
banana pudding (bird) 48
banana slices with honey and raisins (giraffe) 70
carrot and raisin salad (cat) 54
cottage cheese fruit parfait (lamb) 80
dried fruit and nut mix (rat) 108
English muffin meals (Valentine) 128
French toast bites (otter) 94
fresh squeezed orange juice (butterfly) 52
frozen bananas for later use (cow) 60
fruit pizza (rainbow) 130
fruit salad (rabbit) 104
fruit snake (goat) 72

gelatin with pineapple and nuts (rattlesnake) 110
ice cream and strawberries (mouse) 88
lemon-lime fruit salad (flowers) 132
oatmeal cookies with prunes & raisins (hippopotamus) 74
pear and cottage cheese salad (dog) 26
pears with brown sugar and raisins (horse) 74
Waldorf salad (pig) 100

MEAT AND EGGS
beans with corn and hot dogs (alligator) 38
chicken and stuffing (owl) 96
egg salad (Halloween alien) 120
luncheon meat flavor buds (TV character) 34
toothpick snacks (clown) 28

NUTS AND PEANUT BUTTER
chunky peanut butter (clam) 58
cottage cheese fruit parfait (lamb) 80
dried fruit and nut mix (rat) 108
gelatin with pineapple and nuts (rattlesnake) 110
peanut butter coconut candy (football) 118
peanut butter muffins (Thanksgiving turkey) 122
pecan squares (turtle) 114
tuna patties (beaver) 46

VEGETABLES
beans with corn and hot dogs (alligator) 38
bread crumb coating for fish or chicken (koala bear) 78
broccoli topped with bread crumbs and cheese (lion) 84
carrot and raisin salad (cat) 54
carrot chips and pink dip (caterpillar) 56
carrot sticks (skateboard) 138
croutons on salad (seal) 112
cucumbers and tomatoes with dip (frog) 68
jazzed up hamburgers (football player) 30
meatloaf (buffalo) 50
mini stuffed tomatoes or mushrooms (monkey) 86
oatmeal cookies with prunes & carrots (bat) 42
olive and cheese sandwiches (ant) 40
stuffing (owl) 96
toothpick snacks (clown) 28
tuna dip with shredded vegetables (elephant) 64
tuna parties (beaver) 46

Index of Snack Art Foods

alfalfa sprouts 22, 27–28, 76, 132

almonds. 38, 45–46

apple 50, 68, 94, 99–100

bagel 43–44, 97–98

banana 38–39, 45–50, 59–60, 65–66, 69–72, 91–106, 129–130, 132, 152

blueberries. 22, 129–130

bread 22–28, 33–34, 44–46, 49–50, 53–54, 59, 64–66, 77–78, 79–86, 89–90, 92–96, 105–106, 111–118, 125–126, 133–134, 153–154

bun 29–30, 37–38, 75–76

cabbage. 129–130

carrot 24, 27–28, 30, 34, 37–38, 41–42, 45–56, 63–64, 66, 69–70, 75–76, 83–84, 91, 96, 101–104, 109–112, 121–122, 126, 129–130, 137–138

cashews. 121–122

celery 81–82, 131–132

cheese. 24–25, 40, 75, 77, 83–88, 95–96, 136, 154

cheese spread 24, 75–78, 95–96, 133–134

cherries 124, 129–130, 136

coconut. 118, 125–126

corn 37–38

cottage cheese 62, 64, 79–80

cracker 24, 57–58, 64, 93–96, 105–106, 110–114, 122–124

cream cheese 24, 26, 28, 32, 44, 53–54, 72, 79–80, 92, 97–98, 111–112, 125–128, 130, 133

cucumber. 63–64, 67–68

dried fruit. 43–44, 49–50, 59–60, 65–66, 89–90, 105–108, 121–126, 128, 136, 143

egg 46, 50, 94, 114, 119–120, 122, 143, 151

English muffin 127–128

gelatin mix. 139–140

grape 24, 31–32, 38, 40, 43–44, 51–56, 59–61, 65–66, 68, 71–72, 79–80, 89–90, 97–98, 105–108, 111–114, 123–124, 129–130, 135–136, 140, 153–154

green pepper. 29–30, 111–112, 131–132

hot dog. 37–38

kiwi fruit 68, 78, 91–92, 129–130

lettuce 129–132

macadamia nut. 89–90

meat 24, 29–34, 50, 129

mushroom. 77–78, 85–86, 95–96

nori sheet 31–32

nuts 24, 58, 126, 128

olive 24, 26–27, 29–30, 33–34, 39–40, 67–68, 75–78, 83–86, 136

orange 51, 118, 122, 129–130, 136, 151

papaya 71–72, 129–130

peanut 45–46, 73–74, 81–82

peanut butter. 24, 31–32, 45–46, 49–50, 53–54, 57–60, 65–66, 72, 81–82, 89–90, 94, 105–106, 113–114, 117–118, 121–124, 137–138, 143, 153–154, 158

pear 61, 71–74, 91–92, 102–104, 107–108

pecan 41–42, 109–110, 113–114, 121–122

pickle. 37–38

pineapple. 53–54, 109–110

pretzel 49–50, 123, 135–136

prune. 32, 41–44, 97–98, 105–108

puffed rice cereal 24

raisin. 24, 31–32, 34, 44–51, 53–54, 57–61, 65–66, 69–74, 79–82, 91–94, 97–104, 107, 113–114, 117–118, 121, 123, 126, 135–138, 158

rice cake 31–32

sesame seeds. 25, 53–54, 81–82

spinach 131–132

strawberry 25–26, 44, 54, 88, 93–94, 110, 127–130, 135–136

sunflower seeds 24, 53–54, 58, 69–70, 79–80, 87–88, 99–103, 111–112, 119, 121

toasted oat cereal 24, 59–60, 73–74

tomato. 27–28, 67–68, 85–86, 129–130

tuna 46, 64, 154

Vienna sausage 27–28